$\mathcal{T}$rouble on the St. Johns River

"*Trouble on the St Johns River* is a truly inspiring tale of kids taking action against real, current environmental concerns. Jane Wood does a tremendous job of integrating fun, fictional characters, and historical fact and local concerns with just the right amount of suspense and drama."

– **Danielle Dolan,** *Education & Outreach Coordinator*
St. Johns Riverkeeper, Inc.

"*Trouble on the St. John River* is an informative and fact-based book for young readers that will inspire them to get involved in protecting wildlife and their habitats. It's a motivational story about how individuals – including children – CAN and DO make a difference."

– **Patrick M. Rose,** *Aquatic Biologist, Executive Director*
Save the Manatee Club

"Jane Wood's book is an inspiration to the field of environmental education. Her book provides scientifically accurate information that is presented in a child-friendly manner."

– **Alicia B. Marin,** *Senior Educator*
Georgia Sea Turtle Center

"We highly recommend *Trouble on the St. Johns River* to all teachers, parents, students, and young people who care about the St. Johns River and our environment. Jane Wood's book does an outstanding job of highlighting the importance of protecting, as well as, exploring and learning about our natural world. Wood takes the reader on an exciting investigative journey of discovery and enlightenment."

– **Jimmy Orth,** *Executive Director*
St. Johns Riverkeeper, Inc.

"*Trouble on the St. Johns River* not only teaches children of all ages the importance of conservation but that their "green" efforts really can make a difference in keeping our environment clean and healthy for all of its inhabitants."

– **Christy Turner,** *Director of Education*
Museum of Science and History – Jacksonville, Florida

"The story is a good example of how a small group of kids can generate a wave of positive awareness regarding environmental issues."

– **Angie Golubovich,** *Environmental Educator*
Guana Tolomato Matanzas National Estuarine Research Reserve

Also by Jane R. Wood

Voices in St. Augustine

Adventures on Amelia Island:
A Pirate, A Princess, and Buried Treasure

Trouble on the St. Johns River

Jane R. Wood

Florida Kids Press   ◆   Jacksonville, FL

Copyright © 2008 Jane R. Wood

Publisher's Cataloging-In-Publication Data
(Prepared by The Donohue Group, Inc.)

Wood, Jane R., 1947-
Trouble on the St. Johns River / Jane R. Wood.
p. : ill. ; cm.
Includes bibliographical references.

ISBN: 978-0-9792304-4-8

1. Saint Johns River (Fla.)–Juvenile fiction. 2. Environmental protection–Florida–Juvenile
fiction. 3. Rivers–Juvenile fiction. 4. Stream ecology–Juvenile fiction. 5. Saint Johns
River (Fla.)–Fiction. 6. Environmental protection–Florida–Fiction. 7. Rivers–Fiction.
8. Stream ecology–Fiction. I. Title. II. Title: Trouble on the Saint Johns River

PS3573.O59 T76 2008

813.6   2008900487

Library of Congress Control Number: 2008900487

Illustrations, cover design and graphic design by Elizabeth A. Blacker.

Cover photo of manatee © Patrick M. Rose, Save the Manatee Club.

Published through:
Florida Kids Press, 11802 Magnolia Falls Drive
Jacksonville, FL 32258
904-268-9572

♻ Printed and bound in the USA on recycled paper.

To the next generation —

*The one group who surely can "do something"
to make a difference.*

Acknowledgements

In writing this book, I called upon many people to provide me with guidance and assistance. I took my characters to many places so they could learn more about their environment. In visiting those places myself, I connected with some truly dedicated individuals.

My initial research started with Dr. Quinton White, Jr., Professor of Biology & Marine Science and the Dean of the College of Arts & Sciences at Jacksonville University, and the good folks at the St. Johns Riverkeeper. The Riverkeeper, Neil Armingeon; Executive Director, Jimmy Orth; and Education and Outreach Coordinator Danielle Dolan were a constant source of information and enthusiasm for the book.

Janice Nearing, Director of Public Relations for the Save the Manatee Club, patiently responded to my many requests for additional information and support. Executive Director Patrick M. Rose, kindly allowed us to use his amazing underwater photograph of a manatee for our front cover. Angie Golubovich, Environmental Educator at the Guana Tolomato Matanzas National Estuarine Research Reserve, and Alicia B. Marin, Senior Educator at the Georgia Sea Turtle Center, kept me on track with details about their centers and the wonderful educational programs they provide there. Felicia Boyd with the Watershed Action Volunteers; Christy Turner, Director of Education, and John Rouge, Visitor Services Manager, at the Museum of Science and History in Jacksonville were equally supportive.

Special thanks go to Carey Giudici, my editor; Elizabeth Blacker, my graphic designer and good friend; Gena Jerozal, fellow writer and good friend; Linda Smigaj, a very special teacher; and my family members and friends who provided special support, including Terry Wood, Jonathan and Jennifer Fleetwood, Brian Fleetwood, Emily Sutherland, and Manning Lee.

My deepest gratitude goes to my husband, Terry. His constant encouragement and positive support make it all possible.

Chapter 1
Summer Vacation Begins

"Freedom!" Bobby yelled as he ran into the house. As usual he dropped his backpack and various articles of clothing on the floor of the living room and flopped down on the couch. Max, the family dog, joined him and greeted him with a slobbery kiss.

It was the last day of school and he had survived another year. No more homework, no more math problems, no more projects. Nearly three months of escape from anything that resembled schoolwork. *This is heaven*, he thought.

"Bobby, you've left a trail of your things all across the floor," his grandmother said. "You need to pick them up before your mother gets home. Just because you're out of school doesn't mean you can be a slob. Now, scoot!"

Bobby gave her the thumbs-up sign, and she returned

to her baking in the kitchen.

"I think I'm going to hire a maid," he said thoughtfully. "Yes, a maid would be nice. She could bring me food and drink when I watch TV. She could pick up after me and clean my room. She could wash and iron my baseball uniform. An ironed baseball uniform – now that would be sweet!"

"And how are you gonna pay for this maid?" his little sister said. Katy, who had just completed kindergarten and had gotten home earlier, was watching an animal show on TV.

"I haven't figured that out yet…but I will. Don't worry. I will."

He grabbed the remote control and changed the channel.

"Hey, I was watching that!" she said. "Grandma, Bobby's not being nice. He changed the channel in the middle of my show."

Bobby quickly changed the channel back as his grandmother peeked around the kitchen door. She gave him "the evil eye" and pointed to the backpack and clothes that were still on the floor.

"Aw right," he said. "Is this the way it's gonna be all summer? If that's the case, I'm going fishing."

He jumped up from the couch, gathered up his belongings, and threw them into his bedroom. He closed the door quickly. *I'll worry about that later*, he thought.

"Grandma, I'm going fishing. What time do I need to be back for dinner?" he said, as he grabbed a few cookies from the cookie jar and headed toward the garage.

"You can't go fishing by yourself. You know the rules. You've got to wait until your brother gets home, and then see if he'll go with you."

"That's not fair!" he whined. "Everybody treats me like a baby. I'm almost ten." He sat down at the kitchen table, grumbling to himself as he stuffed the cookies into his mouth. His grandmother poured him a glass of milk and patted him on the head.

"You know it's for your own good," she said.

Just then, his grandfather came in through the back door. "What's wrong with him? I figured he'd be a happy camper on the last day of school."

"Bobby wants to go fishing, but I told him he had to wait until Joey came home. He's not very excited about that."

Bobby rolled his eyes because he knew he was probably going to get a lecture on safety. His grandfather was always telling them stories about bad things that happened to people who didn't do things properly.

His grandfather washed his hands in the kitchen sink.

"Tell you what, Sport. Why don't we check out your fishing gear and make sure it's in tip-top shape. You wouldn't want to lose a big one because your line got tangled."

Bobby perked up. He grinned at his grandfather, dusted cookie crumbs from his hands, and headed for the garage.

"There's a whopper of a catfish in that pond and I'm going to catch him this summer," Bobby said. "I bet we could feed the whole family on him."

"I'm not so sure you want to eat a catfish out of one of those ponds," his grandfather said. "The water's pretty dirty, and those catfish are bottom feeders. We could all get mighty sick. If you do catch any fish, the best thing to do would be to release them."

"What do you mean IF? Of course, I'll catch some fish," he said.

They opened the garage door to let the hot Florida air escape and let some light in. Bobby gathered up the fishing poles and tackle box, while his grandfather cleared off a space on the workbench. For the next twenty minutes his grandfather worked on the gear, always explaining what he was doing and then letting Bobby try some of it himself.

"Remember to always check around before you cast. You don't want to hook something or someone."

"Yeah, I know."

"And never go alone. Remember to use the buddy system. That way if one person gets into some kind of trouble, there's another one to help or to go for help."

"Got it," he said. Bobby knew that was the best way to handle these lectures. Actually, his grandfather's advice often came in handy. His grandparents helped out a lot around the house, as his mother wasn't very good at fixing things and making repairs. And they came over on days when she had to be gone and the kids were home. His parents had divorced several years earlier, so his mother welcomed the help.

"Grandpa, how did you learn so many things?"

"Oh, I don't know. It's just things I've picked up over the years." His grandfather finished working on one pole and started on another one. "Plus I read a lot. It's amazing how much you can learn from a book. Hint, hint."

Bobby rolled his eyes again. "I don't intend to read any books this summer. I'm going fishing and swimming and playing baseball and sleeping. I'm not doing anything that resembles schoolwork for three solid months!"

"I hate to hear that," his grandfather said. "You know, there're some great books written about fishing and baseball. You'd be surprised what you can learn from reading a book."

"Yeah, well maybe when I get older. I know all I need to know about those things right now. I'll leave the books and computers to Joey. He likes that kinda stuff."

"And you might learn a few things from your brother. I wish you two would try to get along better. Your mom's got a busy summer writing a story for a national magazine, so your grandmother and I will be spending a lot of time with you kids. I'd like to see you and your brother work on some things together."

"No problem. As long as he stays out of my room, goes fishing with me once a day, and quits trying to boss me around, we'll get along just fine."

His grandfather shook his head sadly. "I can see it's going to be a long summer."

Chapter 2
Something Fishy Going On

Luckily for Bobby, Joey was all in favor of going fishing when he got home.

"You boys be back by 6:00. Your mother will be home by then, and dinner will be ready," their grandmother said.

The boys grabbed a cold water bottle from the refrigerator and their fishing gear from the garage and headed for a pond near the back of their neighborhood. They had been visiting this pond for several years now. Someone had stocked it with fish when they first moved in, and each year the fish got bigger.

They often talked about catching the big catfish rumored to be living on the bottom, but neither of them had actually seen it. Mostly they saw turtles, sometimes a few ducks, and usually lots of mosquitoes.

"Hey, Joey. We should bring your camera with us next time, just in case we catch the monster catfish. No one will believe us if we throw it back."

"That's a good idea," Joey said. "You're not as dumb as you look."

"At least I'm not ugly like you."

And so it went. They exchanged a few more insults as they walked, and then the conversation changed to things about school. Bobby was looking forward to being a 5th grader next year, because he'd be in the oldest group and could boss all the younger kids around. Joey was bemoaning the fact that he'd be a lowly freshman in high school and in the youngest group where he'd be the one getting bossed around.

"Just wait til you go to middle school the next year," he said. "You'll find out."

As they crossed the vacant lot that gave them access to the pond, they stopped dead in their tracks and were struck speechless.

The pond was a cloudy greenish color and was covered with muck. A dozen dead fish floated on top with their mouths wide open. The smell was nauseating.

For a moment they just stood there, taking it all in. "Gross," Bobby said. "What happened?"

"I don't know, but this is not good," Joey said. "Looks like we're not doing any fishing today."

They sat down on the grass and just stared at their favorite fishing hole.

"What should we do?" Bobby finally said.

"I guess we should report this to someone. I don't know who, but maybe Grandpa will know. Let's go home and see what we can find out."

They picked up their poles and started walking back home. Bobby was unusually quiet. But the closer they got to their house, the madder he got. *This was not a good start to his summer vacation. Someone was going to pay for this*, he thought to himself.

He threw his pole down on the grass and burst through the front door, calling for his grandfather.

"Grandpa, where are you?" Bobby shouted. His grandfather was reading the newspaper at the kitchen table.

"You've got to DO something," he said angrily. "Our fishing pond is all yucky and there's dead fish everywhere! We've got to call someone to fix it. There's got to be someone who takes care of these things."

Joey, much calmer, pulled up a chair and explained what they had seen. He told them about a friend of his who had a pond behind his house where a similar thing had happened. He said it was several weeks before they could go near the water again.

"Several weeks!" Bobby said. "The summer will

practically be over by then. We've got to call someone."

"Hold on, son," his grandfather said. "We can look in the phone book for someone to call."

"What do you think it is, Grandpa?" Bobby said.

"Probably too many nutrients from the storm water runoff, fertilizers, pollutants, and natural debris like dead leaves. They all cause algae to grow and algae uses oxygen. When oxygen levels in the water are reduced, fish die."

"Grandpa, you sound like a science book," Bobby said.

"It is basic science. As the algae grow on the surface, it prevents the sunlight from penetrating into the water, which means the plants die — and the fish. Because it's a retention pond, it's probably full of fertilizers and pesticides," his grandfather said. "Now let me look up the number for the Florida Fish and Wildlife Conservation Commission."

"And I'm going to go online and see what I can find," Joey said. "I'll be on the computer. Call me when dinner's ready."

Bobby looked dejected. He felt helpless and useless.

He threw himself on the couch and pouted. Katy walked over to him and patted him on the arm.

"I know how you feel. Remember, when my goldfish died?" she said.

"Yeah, but this is different."

"No, it's not. All creatures deserve to live, even fish. It hurts my feelings when they die," she said. And then to try to make him feel better, she said, "Would you like to change the channel? My show is over." She handed him the remote control.

He changed the channel to a baseball game, but not even that made him feel better. Max, who somehow knew when someone was sad, curled up next to him.

Chapter 3
Let the Investigation Begin

The mood at the dinner table that night was very somber. Their mother had gotten home late, so she had not heard about the pond disaster before they sat down to eat.

"I thought you'd all be excited about the beginning of your summer vacation," she finally said. "Why all the sad faces?"

"It's the dead fish," Katy said.

"I beg your pardon? Dead fish?"

Joey explained the events of the afternoon. Their grandfather added that he had called the Florida Fish and Wildlife Conservation Commission and left a message on the Fish Kill Hotline. Joey said he had gone online and learned some interesting facts about fish kills, water quality, and all kinds of animals.

"Like what kinds of animals?" Katy asked.

"They have information about deer, black bear, Florida panthers, bald eagles, and manatees."

"What's a manatee?' Katy said.

"A manatee is a large gray mammal that lives in the water," Joey said. "It kinda looks like a walrus, but doesn't have any tusks."

"Where do they live?"

"We have manatees here in Florida," her grandfather said. "In fact, we can go over to the County Dock one of these evenings, and we might see some there. They like to feed on the grasses in the shallow water, and I've heard that people see them there all the time."

"Can we do it tonight?" she asked.

"I'm not sure tonight would be good. It looks like it might rain later, and it's not a good idea to be out on the water in case there's lightning," their mother said. "I bet Joey can find you a picture of one on the Internet."

Joey offered to do that right after dinner. Bobby was quiet during most of the discussion until he knocked over his glass of milk. "Oh, great," he said.

16

His mother gave him a quick hug as she wiped up the spilled milk. "Accidents happen. Don't worry about it. It's not the end of the world."

"Fishing was going to be a big part of my world this summer, and now it's not going to happen. Now what am I going to do?"

Their grandmother had not said much all evening. She put her fork down and folded her napkin in her lap and announced that she had an idea.

"It sounds like you kids have stumbled onto something that deserves some attention. Why don't we spend some time this summer learning about how and why these terrible things happen, and what we can do about them?"

There was silence. Then Bobby said, "That sounds like school. I don't want to do anything that smells like schoolwork."

"No, not school. Think of it as an investigation. We'll do some detective work."

"Would we get badges that we could show people and we could ask them questions?" Katy said.

17

"I think we'll ask lots of questions, but we won't need badges," she said. "Bobby, you started it already with your first question — who do we call to fix the problem at the pond? Grandpa made a phone call and Joey got some information from the Internet."

She looked around the table. Katy was interested, but Bobby looked skeptical. "Why don't we actually visit some places where we can learn about fish and animals and how to protect them?" Grandma said.

"Like where?" Bobby said. He was not impressed with this idea. It sounded too much like a school field trip where you had to listen to someone talk about things and then write a paper about it when you got back to school.

"I know one," his grandfather said. "We could go to the Guana Tolomato Matanzas National Estuarine Research Reserve. It's not far from here, and I see in the newspaper that they have programs at their education center all the time. I bet we could find one that you'd like, Bobby. And I think they even allow fishing out there."

"Do they have manatees there? I want to see one for

real, not just a picture," Katy said.

"I don't know, but we can find out. And if they don't have them there, we'll find out where we can see some. Now, how does that sound?"

Katy was excited. "I like your idea, Grandma. I think it will be fun."

Joey agreed with Katy. Bobby was still not convinced, but agreed to go along.

"If we can't go fishing, we might as well do something," he said.

"Great," his grandfather said. "I'll see what I can find out about some of the programs they have for kids."

"Just make sure we don't have to write any reports," Bobby said.

Chapter 4
Learning about Manatees

After dinner, Joey retreated to the spare bedroom that served as an office and sometime guest room. He wanted to check out some Web sites on the Internet and find some pictures of manatees for Katy.

His first search led him to the official Web site of the *Save the Manatee Club*. It had underwater photographs of the large sea creatures swimming in crystal clear water. Sometimes there were two of them together and even one of a mother with her baby. He learned that the average male manatee can weigh more than 1,000 pounds. *That's half a ton*, he thought in amazement.

Other Web sites offered even more information. He discovered that the West Indian manatee, the kind found in Florida, can live to be sixty years old. They have no natural enemies, but many die of causes related to

21

human beings. Because they are slow-moving, many get fatal injuries from collisions with boats. Others die from eating or getting caught in fishing line, crab traps, or litter. New construction, the dredging of waterways, and water pollution also contribute to their deaths by diminishing the quality of their natural habitats and making it harder for them to find food. He read that there are about 3,000 manatees left in the United States.

Soon Katy wandered in. "Did you find me a manatee?" she said.

"Sure did. Wanna see?" She nodded and crawled up into his lap.

She stared at the big gray creatures as Joey scrolled through many of the photographs. She smiled when she saw the picture of the mother with her baby. Joey explained some of the things he had read about them, leaving out the parts about how so many of them are killed every year.

Then Bobby came into the room, looking like he'd lost his best friend. "What are ya doin?" he said.

"We're learning about manatees," Katy said. "Come

look. Aren't they cute?"

He looked at the computer screen and made a frown. "Those are the ugliest things I've ever seen."

"No, they're not," Katy said. "I bet they think you're pretty ugly."

"Well, if I ever bump into one, I'm going to go the other way."

"That's a good idea," Joey said. "Because it's illegal to touch them or feed them. It could cost you up to $500 and 60 days in jail."

"Why?" Katy said. "Why can't you feed them?"

Joey explained that it's illegal to feed many wild creatures, because it makes them too comfortable around humans.

"Unfortunately not all people are nice," he said. "The laws are made to protect them."

"You mean people would try to hurt them – on purpose?" she asked.

Joey looked at Bobby. They both felt sad that Katy had to think about things like that. She was very sensitive, especially when it came to animals. Fortunately their mother came in the room. She noticed immediately that things were kind of tense.

"Mom, why would people want to hurt manatees?" Katy asked.

Jennifer Johnson looked at her sons, now recognizing why they seemed so uncomfortable. They were both very protective of their little sister, and it seemed more and more that Katy was asking questions they didn't know how to answer.

"Well, Sweetie, I don't know. There are just some bad people in this world,"she said. She paused, trying to find the right words that would alert her daughter to danger-ous people without scaring her. "We need to be aware that those kinds of people exist. That's why you should never talk to strangers."

"But what about animals? They don't know who's good and who's bad?"

"That's why we have laws. Hopefully it will discour-age people from doing bad things to animals. And if they don't, then the law can deal with them."

"But what if there's no police around?"

24

"Then it's up to others to let the police know."

"I'll save the day," Bobby shouted, as he jumped up on the bed. He was throwing fists in the air, kick boxing his legs, and roaring like a lion. "Bad guys, beware!"

Joey groaned and rolled his eyes. Katy giggled and cheered. And their mother shook her head.

"When you're done saving the world, please remake the bed. Or I'll have to report you for disorderly conduct."

"Yes, ma'am," he said and saluted her.

"I'm going to be working on this big project for most of the summer, so you're going to be spending a lot of time with your grandparents. I don't want to get any bad reports. You understand?" she said, looking directly at Bobby.

"Loud and clear. Over and out," he said with another salute.

"Good. Now that's enough talk about bad guys. Who wants popcorn? Let's start this summer off right."

Chapter 5
The Next Generation

On their first day of summer vacation, the kids slept in. Bobby had baseball practice in the afternoon, and Katy went to play at a friend's house. Joey stayed on the computer most of the day. He played some games and e-mailed his friend Barby in Boston. Barby's school was still in session for another week, so he wouldn't get any response from her until that evening. He had met her at the end of the previous summer when they were both touring a historic house in St. Augustine. They exchanged e-mail addresses that day and had been communicating ever since.

The next day the kids and the grandparents were on their way to their first investigation.

"We're going to the Guana Tolomato Matanzas National Estuarine Research Reserve," their grandfather said. "Try saying that three times fast."

"Grandpa, what's a reserve?" Katy said.

He explained that a reserve is a protected area along a coastal region. Biologists use them for research and to do restoration projects to return those areas to their natural conditions.

"This Reserve has thousands of acres of protected woods, marshes, mangroves, and wetlands. Birds, animals, fish, shellfish, and plants can live there undisturbed by man.

"The part of this Research Reserve that we're going to is located north of St. Augustine and includes a recreation area and an education center. Today we're going to the Environmental Education Center," their grandfather explained.

As they drove east toward the ocean, they saw many trucks and lots of construction equipment entering and leaving the road. Many new homes were being built there.

"I remember when this was all woods," Joey said. "Pretty soon all the trees will be gone."

"What happens to all the animals when the woods are gone?" Katy asked.

"That's a good question," their grandmother said. "We see stories in the news all the time about animals that show up in populated areas because they're losing more and more of their natural habitat. Sometimes bears end up in neighborhoods looking for food."

"That's not fair," Katy said. "Doesn't anybody do anything to help them?"

"There are laws and regulations that protect them somewhat. For example, if there's a nest of certain endangered birds on a piece of property that's going to have some construction on it, the builders may have to establish a buffer zone or wait until the baby birds hatch and leave the nest. "

She told them another story about gopher tortoises. If a company wants to construct a new building and there are gopher tortoises on the property, they have to move them. But first they have to get a permit to move them, because they are a threatened species. And sometimes scientists have to catch the tortoises and move them to a new place.

"I agree with Katy," Bobby said. "That doesn't seem fair. The animals were there first."

"Well, it's the age-old problem that comes with progress," their grandfather said. "People have got to live somewhere. We've just got to figure out ways to live together that is friendly to both the animals and to the earth. I think you're going to find that situations like the dead fish in your fishing pond are just one example of things that are happening all over the world. We've got to be better protectors of the earth, or the next generation is going to be in serious trouble."

"That's us, Grandpa," Joey said. "We're the next generation."

And the car grew very quiet.

Chapter 6
Bald Eagles and Beach Mice

They arrived at the Environmental Education Center a little before noon. As they entered the exhibit area, their eyes traveled upward to a model of a large whale suspended from the ceiling. There were many other exhibits they wanted to check out, but their grandfather told them they were going to attend the monthly Brown Bag Lunch Lecture that would begin shortly. They could see everything after the lecture, he said.

"Oh no!" Bobby said. "Did you say lecture?"

"Hush," his grandmother said. "Your grandfather called ahead and found out this will fit right in with what we've been talking about. I packed each of us a lunch, and I put some of your favorites in your bag. And no, you don't have to write any reports."

She urged everyone to visit the restroom before they

entered the auditorium.

"I'll take Katy out and show her the exhibits if she gets bored," she told the boys. "This might be a little over her head."

There were already many people in the room. Some had started eating their lunches. They found five seats together in the second row. There was a large screen in the front of the room, and several people in official-looking shirts were talking with some of the visitors.

Soon the lights dimmed and the program began.

One of the staff members talked about the different species of wildlife monitored at the Research Reserve. She talked about sea turtles, gopher tortoises, the striped newt, and various birds like the bald eagle, the peregrine falcon, and numerous shore birds. She also told them about the Anastasia Island Beach Mouse which is on the endangered species list.

"The only place in the world where this mouse exists naturally is on and around Anastasia Island just south of here. There are also some at the Fort Matanzas National Monument near the island, but if a bad hurricane hit that area directly, we could lose the whole species."

She showed pictures of the mouse on the large screen. It had white markings on its nose, face, and belly, but was sand-colored on its back.

Katy was enchanted. She threw her hand in the air.

"Yes, do you have a question?" the speaker said.

"Yes, ma'am. Is anybody trying to save them?"

"Yes, we are. Several years ago we captured some of them in traps, and brought them to the Reserve, hoping to start a colony here. We tagged them with little earring tags so we could track them. Unfortunately, their numbers still seem to be low. But we can always hope."

Katy sat back in her chair and shoved her lunch away. She had a very serious look on her face. Joey smiled at his grandparents and patted Katy on the head.

The speaker started talking about sea turtles. She showed pictures of some loggerhead turtles crawling up the beach to lay their eggs. She told them how important it is to educate people not to disturb the turtles when they come ashore.

"Do not shine flashlights as it may cause the females to abandon the nesting process," she said. "And we ask residents along the ocean to turn off their outside lights at night. The lights can disorient the hatchlings, and they may go in the wrong direction away from the water."

She explained that sea turtle patrol volunteers check for new nests every morning during the nesting season. They collect information on the nests and help protect the hatchlings from predators and humans.

At the end of her lecture, she talked about some things they could all do to help protect the environment and the animals. Many organizations sponsored clean-up days, when volunteers pick up trash along the beaches. She warned that plastic items, like soda can plastic rings, balloons, plastic bags, and fishing line should all be disposed of properly. Animals, birds, turtles, fish, and manatees can get tangled up in these, and often eat them by mistake, she said.

Katy raised her hand again.

"Do you have any manatees here?" she asked.

"Yes, we do, but it's hard to predict when and where

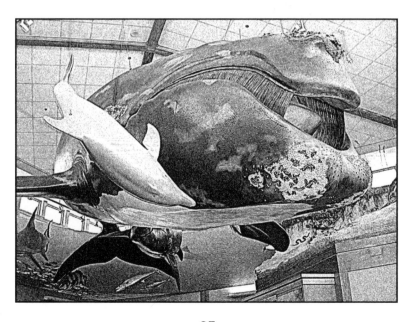

they're going to show up. This year we've had a record number spotted in Northeast Florida, which is very encouraging," she said.

"And on that positive note, my lecture is over. Please feel free to ask me more questions, and by all means, visit our interpretive exhibit area. Also, there are telescopes along the back of the center where you can check out the bald eagle's nest just across the water. Thanks for coming."

Bobby wanted to see the eagle's nest and was already rushing out of the room. Joey held Katy's hand as they walked toward the exhibit area.

When the kids were out of sight, the grandparents gave each other a high five. "Well done, Grandma," their grandfather said. "Well done."

Chapter 7
The Education Center

Bobby went straight to the telescopes to look for the eagle's nest. Katy was drawn to the aquariums. She saw several kinds of fish and a turtle that kept looking at her. Joey was checking out a display on Migrations. It had information about whales, turtles, birds, manatees, and manta rays.

Their grandfather went outside to join Bobby. "See anything?"

"Yeah. Look over there across the water at that tall tree," he said pointing. "You can see a nest at the very top, and there's an eagle sitting in the tree next to it."

His grandfather looked through the telescope. "What a magnificent creature," he said, and then took another look. The others came outside to join them. Bobby pointed to the tree, and showed them where to focus the telescope.

"I wonder if there are any babies in the nest," Katy said.

"Maybe we should ask someone," their grandmother said. "We could buy a book about eagles, and you could learn more about them."

Bobby looked at his grandfather. "You put her up to that, didn't you?"

"Nope. She came up with that all on her own."

Joey had brought his digital camera. He tried to take

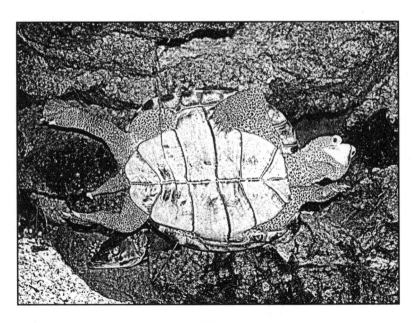

38

a picture of the nest, but it was too far away, so he took some shots of the river and some snowy egrets that were wading in the water not far from them.

Back inside, they watched a short film about the Reserve. They were able to see how big the Reserve is and learned about its ten miles of hiking trails. They also learned about other activities like kayaking, fishing, and bird watching.

Then the boys got a scavenger hunt sheet full of questions to answer after studying the exhibits. As usual, the boys made a competition out of it, seeing who could get the most answers. They read the displays and opened many of the Discovery Drawers which contained things like fossils, crabs, and sharks' teeth.

Katy focused her attention on a life-size replica of a sea turtle suspended from the ceiling.

"Grandpa, can we go see some sea turtles some day?" she asked.

"It just so happens that there's a Sea Turtle Center on Jekyll Island, just north of here. Maybe we can make a run up there as part of our summer investigations."

"That would be cool," she said. "I think they're cute."

Joey took some pictures of the different exhibits and then they visited the Nature Store. Joey bought a book on marine mammals. Katy got a sea turtle t-shirt, and Bobby picked out a small furry stuffed manatee. He was a little embarrassed about getting a stuffed toy, so he added a rubber snake just so no one would make fun of him.

"That was fun, Grandma," Katy said as they got in the car to leave. "Thank you for bringing us."

"Yeah, it wasn't bad," Bobby added. "Even if it was educational."

Joey mumbled his thanks, already reading his new book.

Chapter 8
Right Whales

That night when Joey went online to check his e-mail, he found one from Barby saying her family may be visiting Florida again. Her father had been invited to a conference in St. Augustine, and her parents were looking for a condo on the beach for a week. Joey was extremely excited about seeing her again, but was also a little scared.

What if she doesn't like me, he thought. He always had time to think about what he wanted to say to her in e-mails, but having to talk to her face-to-face was an entirely different situation. What would they talk about? *This could be a disaster,* he thought.

Of course, he replied to her e-mail that he was glad she might be coming back to Florida, but deep inside he had some serious doubts about it. She said they would know in a few days if it was going to happen.

41

In the meantime, he decided to focus on learning all he could about manatees and other wildlife in their area. At least he could maintain his image with Katy. She thought he was brilliant, but it was getting harder and harder to answer all her questions.

Their grandfather had promised to take them fishing the next day and told them there was a possibility they could see some manatees. Joey wanted to be prepared with as much information as possible.

Their plans to get an early start on fishing the next day changed when a thunderstorm blew through. It rained throughout the morning, but the weather reports said it would clear up by evening.

"We'll give it a shot later," their grandfather said. "We'll go right after we eat an early dinner. It will be cooler then too. I already cleared it with your mother, as she has to work late tonight."

They watched the movie *Free Willy* on TV that afternoon. Katy asked several questions about whales. Bobby made threats about what he'd do if he caught someone picking on a whale, but Joey pointed out that there weren't any whales in the St. Johns River.

"We do get North Atlantic right whales off the coast of Florida during the winter months, usually between December and March," their grandfather said. "They come here to give birth because the waters are warmer. Then they go back to the North Atlantic in March. However, I heard somewhere that sometimes a few strays don't know the rules so they stay a little longer."

"Grandpa, how do you know so much?" Katy asked.

"I read a lot," he said, and winked at Bobby. "And I watch a lot of documentaries on television."

"I've always wanted to go on a whale-watching cruise," Grandma said. "Maybe one of these days, I will."

"Can I go too?" Katy said.

"We'll see. That would be fun, wouldn't it?"

Chapter 9
Fishing at County Dock

As promised, they ate an early dinner. By 6:30 they had loaded up the car with all their fishing gear and were off to the County Dock. They drove down a tree-lined dirt road that ended at a small boat ramp for launching boats into the river. In addition to a long dock that extended out into the river, there was a park with paths cut through the trees. A wooden walkway had been built along the waterfront, so people could enjoy the natural environment without disturbing the plants or the animals.

Bobby bolted out of the car and ran toward the dock. He ran back to the car, urging the others to hurry.

"I've been waiting all week to go fishing, and I'm not waiting any longer."

They were used to Bobby's outbursts. They had learned long ago that sometimes it was easier to go along

45

with him than to fight the inevitable. The boys gathered up the fishing gear, while Katy and her grandmother applied some mosquito repellent.

As they walked down the long pier, Bobby stopped to ask each of the people fishing if they had caught anything. One man had a bucket with several mullet sloshing around in it. He was casting a net from the dock. Another man was wading in the shallow water with his casting net and looked like something out of the Bible.

Katy and her grandmother walked to the end of the dock and asked the boys fishing there if they had seen any manatees. A lady wearing a large straw hat told them there had been one there earlier in the week, but she hadn't seen any lately. The lady had a bucket and several small bottles she was dipping into the water.

"What are you doing?" Katy asked.

"I'm taking water samples," she said.

"What for?"

"I'm testing the quality of the water to see how clear it is and how much dissolved oxygen it has in it."

"Why?"

"It can give us some warning signs if there's a problem developing."

"What kind of problem?"

"We can detect early signs of algae blooms. They threaten fish, plants, and people. We can also measure the levels of salt and acid in the water."

She went on to explain that in the summer of 2005 there had been a terrible situation when the river was covered with a green gooey mess for about a hundred miles. It was caused by too many nutrients going into the water from yard fertilizers, pesticides, and discharges from factories and businesses.

"They called it the Green Monster and they even did a television show about it," she said.

Katy was very curious about what the lady was doing and asked if she could help. Her grandmother stood nearby, letting Katy discover these new things on her own. After Katy left to join her brothers, Grandma talked with the woman and found out she was doing all these tests as a volunteer with a program called *Watershed Action Volunteers*. She said they report their findings to the

St. Johns River Water Management District.

"We can always use more volunteers — you ought to think about getting involved," she suggested.

"I might just do that," Grandma said. "My husband would probably enjoy it too. But today we're being grandparents, so I'd better get back to the kids." She thanked the lady for taking so much time to answer all of Katy's questions, and then joined the others.

Bobby had picked a fishing spot where no one else was standing.

"I'm going to catch a big one. I can feel it," he said.

"All I feel is hot and sweaty. I hope it cools off when the sun goes down," Joey said.

Their grandfather helped them get set up. They cast their lines into the water and waited. And waited. And waited.

"It's too calm. Maybe we should go somewhere else," Bobby said.

"Patience, Bobby," his grandfather said. "You've got to be patient."

Just then one of the other fishermen reeled in a huge

catfish. Bobby set down his pole and ran down to see it. He came back with a big smile on his face.

"I'm next," he said. "Just watch me."

Katy sat down next to them, dangling her feet over the edge. She told them in great detail all of the things she had learned from the lady taking the water samples.

They fished for another half hour, enjoying the quiet of the river and watching a variety of birds catching their dinners. When it started to get dark, their grandfather said it was time for them to go home.

"But I haven't caught anything yet," Bobby said.

"Well, that's the way it goes sometimes," he replied. "We can come back another time."

Bobby reluctantly reeled in his line. He said he wanted to walk to the end of the dock before leaving. He walked slowly toward the end, passing the boys who had been fishing there. They were calling it quits and hadn't caught anything either, but that didn't make Bobby feel any better.

He stood there for a few minutes watching a boat speed by in the distance, wishing he had a boat so he could fly across the water, too. He didn't notice the disturbance in the water directly below where he was standing. Suddenly a loud "Whosh" sound made him jump back in surprise. He looked down and saw a large gray snout with short whiskers peering up at him. At first, he was too startled to do anything. But when he realized what it was, he dropped to his knees to get a closer look.

The creature was about six feet long and its large flippers were stirring up the water. It nosed around the pilings of the dock and then dove back underwater and disappeared.

It happened so fast he didn't even have time to call to the others. He walked around the end of the dock, hoping to catch sight of it again, but it was gone. And then he thought of Katy.

"Katy, quick, come here. I just saw a manatee."

Katy and the rest of them came running. He pointed to the water where the manatee had been, but all was now calm.

"It was right here just a minute ago," he said. "It was the biggest thing I ever saw."

The others could tell by the expression on his face that he was not making this up. He started pacing up and down the dock, looking for more stirrings in the water.

"What did it look like?" Katy said.

"It was incredible. It looked just like the pictures on the Internet, but only bigger." He put his hands on his hips and shook his head.

"This is the best fishing trip ever. And I didn't even catch anything!"

Chapter 10
Museum of Science and History

It was several days before they could go fishing again. On the evenings that Bobby didn't have baseball games, it rained. On one of the rainy afternoons, they visited the Museum of Science and History in downtown Jacksonville. They especially wanted to see the Atlantic Tails exhibit which featured whales, manatees, and dolphins. It had life-size models of the sea creatures, including a huge right whale mounted on one wall. The kids enjoyed the hands-on exhibits and Katy finally got to see a manatee, even if it wasn't a real one.

Bobby was gaining a new appreciation for the information on many of the displays. He read them all. He had also stopped teasing his brother about being a computer geek, and asked him to find some things on the Internet when they got home. His close encounter with a live manatee had captured his imagination, and he wanted to learn more.

They spent several more hours in the museum, also visiting the exhibits on dinosaurs and some species of animals that live in Florida. Katy did not like the snakes, so she and her grandmother hurried on to the regional history display. It showed the early Timucuan Indians, the Great Fire of Jacksonville of 1901, and the inside of a house of the 1950s.

"This is like the Museum of History on Amelia Island," Katy said. "We visited it when we were there on spring break. I like looking at the way things used to be."

"I remember many of those things they've got in that house," her grandmother told her. "I guess I belong in a museum, too." They both laughed.

Before going home, they went to see a show in the Planetarium. The night sky over Florida was projected on the dome-shaped ceiling. A staff member pointed out the various stars, planets, and constellations.

After the show, they visited the gift shop where they each bought a book, even Bobby. Katy bought one filled with paper dolls wearing old-fashioned clothes. Bobby got one that had manatees in it. And Joey selected one on astronomy.

On their way back to the car, Katy spotted the huge fountain behind the museum near the river. Its large spires of water shot high into the air like a whale spout.

"I wanna go see the fountain," she said. They followed her lead like baby ducks after the mama duck. Joey took a picture of the Jacksonville skyline looking through the water spray of the fountain. He also took a photo of Katy with their grandparents. He thought it might make a good Christmas present for his grandparents. He always had trouble coming up with ideas for them at Christmas.

Bobby wandered over to the Riverwalk that bordered the river. Several people were strolling or jogging along the wooden walkway. He noticed a large boat on pontoons loaded with people. It said River Taxi on the side, but it wasn't coming from across the river where the water taxis usually went. It had come from the south. He walked over to where it was docking.

About forty people got off the boat. Most had cameras

and some were carrying notebooks. A man with a long white beard, a grey pony tail, and a khaki baseball cap shouted goodbyes to the group.

"Don't forget, next time we'll go up the Cedar River," he said.

The man gathered up a satchel, slung it over his shoulder and stepped ashore.

"See you next month, Barney," he said to the man driving the boat. "Thanks for spotting those manatees. That was a special treat for those students." He started walking toward the parking lot.

"Hey, Mister. Can I talk to you for a minute?" Bobby said.

The man stopped. "Sure, what do you need?"

"I saw a manatee this week, and I'd like to see some more. Where did this boat go?"

"We went up river, that's south, because the St. Johns flows north, and took a nature tour of the river. Those were students from an environmental studies class at the college. They wanted to see some sources of major pollution, and I'm the man who knows where they are. My name is Neil, and I'm the Riverkeeper."

"Hi, I'm Bobby Johnson," and he thrust out his hand to shake hands.

"What's a Riverkeeper?" he said.

"Well, I'm kind of a watchdog who looks out for the river. I'm part of a group of people who work to improve the water quality in the St. Johns River. We try to educate people about the issues that impact our waterways. That's why I was with that group of students today. We try to teach them early."

Bobby thought about that for a moment. Just then his grandfather walked up. Bobby remembered he wasn't supposed to talk to strangers.

"Uh, Grandpa. This is Neil, the Riverkeeper. He's like a scientist who keeps an eye on the river."

"Yes, I've read about your organization in the newspaper. That's some mighty fine work you do for the community," Grandpa said. He shook Neil's hand.

"He takes people on nature tours in that boat. Can we go sometime?" Bobby asked.

"We'll have to find out more about it," he said. "Is the

trip appropriate for kids? We've got three grandkids, and I'd like for all three of them to be able to go."

"Of course. We have a Family River Ride you might be interested in," and he handed Grandpa a business card. "Just call my office for the summer schedule. We'd love to have you join us – all of you. I need to be getting back to the office, but we'll look forward to your call."

"Thanks, Mister,"Bobby said enthusiastically. Neal headed for the parking lot, and Bobby and his grandfather turned to join the others. "Can we really go?"he said.

"I'll call them tomorrow. Let's go tell the others."

Chapter 11
A New Family Member

The next day they called to schedule the river tour. In the meantime, Joey went online to check out the Web site of the St. Johns Riverkeeper. He learned that the St. Johns River is the longest river in Florida and flows north. Near the mouth of the river at Jacksonville it mixes fresh-water with salt water from the ocean, making it a rich estuary for birds, plants, and water animals.

Joey also discovered there are more than 160 River-keeper organizations throughout the world. The concept of "keepers" assigned to protect the streams and rivers goes back to the Middle Ages. Their goals are the same today – to protect the quality of the local waterways.

He also found a phone number to report a manatee sighting. He told Bobby about it, and suggested he call the number to report the manatee he had seen at the

County Dock. Bobby said he would do that and felt a real sense of importance.

Another Web page talked about *River Friendly Yards*. When he mentioned it at dinner that night, his mother suggested they create a Wildlife Habitat in their backyard.

"I remember when I wrote a story about a local garden club. They had a guest speaker who talked about backyard habitats. He said you need to landscape with plants that require less water. And if you plant colorful flowers, they will attract butterflies, bees, and birds," she said. "I bet you could find something about that on the Internet. Want to check that out for me?"

Joey said he would.

"I like butterflies and birds. Can I help?" Katy said.

"It's *may* I help. And yes, I think we can all help. Your grandmother has a green thumb. She'd probably love to do this."

"Grandma has a green thumb?" Katy said, as she wrinkled her nose.

They all laughed. Katy looked embarrassed and gave her brothers a dirty look.

"That's just a phrase we use for people who are good at growing things," her mother said. "I've never been very good with plants, but Grandma's a real gardener."

Katy told them to be careful with the kinds of fertilizers they used because some are bad for the river. She told them what the lady at the County Dock had told her about the Green Monster and that they all needed to do their part so that would never happen again. She thought they should tell all their neighbors about it, too.

Katy often surprised them with her insights. They exchanged quick glances at each other as Katy finished her macaroni and cheese. When dinner was over, Jennifer asked about the river tour they were going to take with the Riverkeeper.

"I'm looking forward to it," Bobby said. "The last group saw several manatees. I'm hoping we'll see some, too."

"Me, too," said Katy. "I missed seeing the last one. And maybe we'll see some dolphins, too."

"If I can break away from the project I'm working on next week, I'll join you. Sounds like a great trip," Jennifer said. "And we might want to plan a trip to Blue Spring

State Park when it gets cooler. I hear dozens of manatee go there during the winter."

"Cool,"Bobby said.

Joey reminded them they could adopt a manatee if they wanted to.

"They even have photos of manatees for adoption on the *Save the Manatee* Web site,"he said.

"You mean I could have a manatee for a brother?" Bobby said.

"Not exactly. You pick out a manatee, send in $25, and they send you a picture of it and some details about its life,"he said. "You even get an adoption certificate."

"Can we, Mom? Can we adopt a manatee?" Katy begged.

"I think that would be a good idea. But I'd like to see you kids earn the money to adopt one. That way, it would truly be yours. Twenty-five dollars is not a lot. Don't go asking Grandma and Grandpa for it either. I think this is something you need to do by yourselves."

The room got very quiet. Bobby looked at Joey and then at Katy. They all grinned at each other and shook their heads in agreement.

Then Katy said, "I've got some money in my piggy bank."

"And I can sell a few of my baseball cards," Joey added. "I bet we could do some yard work for Grandma and Grandpa. That would be OK, wouldn't it, Mom?"

"Yes, that would be fine. There might be some other neighbors you can do some odd jobs for, too. And we could do a garage sale and get rid of some toys you no longer play with."

They all agreed. Joey said he'd print off the forms needed to adopt a manatee so they'd know what to do. Katy said she wanted to pick a girl manatee to adopt. And Bobby said he couldn't wait to tell all his friends they were adopting a sister who had whiskers and weighed half a ton.

"And if we're lucky, we might be able to meet your new sister one of these days. We'll have to plan that trip to Blue Spring State Park this winter," their mother said.

The room got quiet as they imagined what that would be like.

Chapter 12
Raising Money

They spent the next morning planning how they were going to earn the money needed to adopt a manatee. Katy counted the money in her piggy bank. It totaled $4.38. She said she would give some of it, but wanted to keep some to buy flowers for the backyard habitat.

"I want to be good to the butterflies too, you know."

Joey went through some baseball cards, and picked out a few.

"I hate to sell too many now. They'll be worth much more in the future. That would give me more money to donate to some good cause then,"he said. "I'll see if I can mow some lawns or watch somebody's pets when they go out of town."

Bobby was sorting through his toys in his room. He had a stack for ones to keep, and another stack for ones to give away. The problem was that all the toys were in the stack to keep. Then he stumbled on something that he thought was the perfect solution. He found a microscope that his Aunt Mary had given them on one of her visits. She was a biology teacher and liked showing them things under the microscope.

He took it out of the case to make sure it was not broken, and then realized that it might be good to have this if they wanted to examine some of the water samples, like that lady had done at County Dock. *We could do our own water testing*, he thought.

When Joey came into Bobby's room, he immediately realized the problem.

"It's not as easy as it looks, is it?" he said.

"No. I don't want to get rid of any of these things. I'd even forgotten about some of them. But now that I know they're there, I want to keep them," Bobby said.

They were looking very dejected when it was time for lunch.

"Why the long faces?" their grandfather said.

Joey answered. "We're trying to earn some money so

we can adopt a manatee. Mom says we have to earn it ourselves – you can't give it to us. We thought about doing a garage sale, but we don't have much to sell."

"Well, you can't have a sale without something to sell, can you?" their grandfather said.

Just then Katy spoke up. "I have something to sell."

"And what would that be?" Joey asked.

"I'm going to have a lemonade stand on Saturday, and me and Grandma are going to make some oatmeal cookies to sell," she said very matter-of-factly.

"Grandma and I," her grandmother corrected her.

Both boys looked at Katy in amazement. She was way ahead of them, and could probably earn the whole $25 by herself. They were embarrassed.

"That's a great idea," their grandfather said. "I bet you boys could do that, too."

"Ah, you mean bake and sell cookies?" Bobby said. "I don't think so!"

"No, I have a better idea," he said. "Why don't you do a car wash in the driveway at the same time that Katy has her lemonade stand. I'll be your first customer. I'll pay you $10 to wash my car. I'll give you another dollar, if you vacuum it out. You know how messy Grandma is when she eats in the car," he said with a wink.

"I heard that!" Grandma said. "No dessert for you, Mister."

Bobby and Joey thought about it for a minute. "This could work," Joey said.

"Yeah, and we can hope that it doesn't rain before Saturday," Bobby said. "In fact, you know that big mud puddle that's on the main road just before you turn into our street? Maybe we could go add some more mud to it when no one's looking."

They all laughed.

"I don't think that's such a good idea," their grandfather said. "A better way to drum up some business would be to print some fliers and distribute them to the neighbors. If you tell them why you're trying to earn the money, you'll probably get some takers. People like to help a good cause."

"Yeah, I see what you mean," Joey said. "C'mon Bobby, let's make a flier. We could even put a picture of a manatee on it."

"First, you're going to finish your sandwich," their grandmother said. "And Bobby, you need to check your baseball schedule. You may have a game on Saturday."

"Right-o," he said.

When they had finished their lunch, Katy and Grandma made a grocery shopping list so they'd have all the ingredients for the cookies and lemonade. Grandma offered to pay for the ingredients as her donation to the cause.

"Grandma, can we stop by that garden store, so I can see how much the flowers are going to cost for our backyard?" Katy said.

"Sure. But let's plan what we're going to do first. When you start a project like this, you need to have a plan."

"This is going to be fun, Grandma," Katy said.

"I think so too," she replied.

Chapter 13
Birds and Butterflies

Katy and her grandmother studied the information Joey had printed off the Web site for the *National Wildlife Federation* about attracting birds, butterflies, and other wildlife.

"Your backyard will be perfect for this," Grandma said. "You've already got some trees, some of the plants they recommend, and a bird bath. The bird bath is important because birds need clean water. We probably need to give it a good cleaning though."

"But we don't have any bird houses," Katy said. "Can we buy one?"

"Why don't you ask your grandfather to build you one? He can use some of the wood scraps he has in his workshop. That way, we'd be recycling, as well."

"I like that idea. I could help him. What else do we

need?" Katy asked.

Her grandmother started drawing a sketch of their backyard, showing the boundary lines, the back fence, and all the trees and shrubs. She explained that it was important to have trees and shrubs for birds for nesting and raising their young. They also provide protection from their predators, she said.

"I think that tall oak tree in the back will be just perfect for a bird feeder. We'll try to find one that is squirrel-proof."

"I like squirrels," Katy protested. "Why don't you want them around?"

"They can be real rascals. They'll eat it all if given the opportunity," Grandma said. "Besides, the squirrels will drive Max crazy. He watches them from the sliding glass door when they come into the yard, and barks like a mad dog."

"He just thinks he's protecting us," Katy said defensively.

"Yes, I know, but he'll also scare away the birds. We just need to be careful how we go about this. We don't want a war going on between the species."

Grandma read some more of the recommendations about being certified as a Wildlife Habitat. She suggested they ask Grandpa to find a place for a compost pile.

"What's that?" Katy said.

"Compost is made up of grass clippings, leaves, and even kitchen waste, like potato peelings and coffee grounds. They're all put together in a pile, then turned over at least once a week with a rake or shovel. When it decomposes, it makes a rich mixture that you put around your plants. It helps plants stay healthy, adds nutrients to the soil, and helps keep moisture in the soil. It's a great way to recycle organic materials, and cut down on commercial fertilizers and pesticides that hurt the environment."

"That's perfect," Katy said. "Remember what the lady at the County Dock said about being careful with too many fertilizers." Then she studied the drawing carefully. Her grandmother continued to add things to the sketch of the garden.

"But where do the flowers go?" Katy asked.

73

"We'll put some right here," her grandmother said as she drew some stick flowers in front of the azalea bushes and some more around the oak tree. "Butterflies need plants with nectar, and they like bright colors, like reds and purples and yellows."

"Can I choose the flowers?" Katy said.

"I think that's a great idea. I'll help you find ones that are easy to maintain. We want our garden to be earth-friendly and need as little water as possible. We're only supposed to water twice a week now, so we should select plants that don't need a lot of water."

"Grandma, you're very smart. I'm glad you're in my family."

"Me too, Katy. Me too."

Chapter 14
Going Green

Saturday was a beautiful sunny day. And fortunately, several neighbors were having garage sales so there was lots of activity in the neighborhood.

The boys had created a flier on their computer that advertised their car wash and lemonade stand. They had taken copies around to most of the homes in their neighborhood, and one of the ladies having a garage sale offered to give a flier to each person who bought something from her.

Grandpa had been right about including some information about using the money they earned to adopt a manatee. Several of the neighbors commented that even if they didn't need a car wash on Saturday, they would make a donation.

"Cool," Bobby said. "If we're lucky, we won't even

have to work for it."

Everyone in the family helped them get set up that morning. Joey and Grandpa carried a table out to the front yard. Grandma put a red and white checked table cloth over the table, and their mother placed a vase of flowers on it.

"That will make it look nice," she said.

Katy and Bobby had made a sign from a large cardboard box they found in the garage. "Lemonade and Cookies For Sale. 50 cents a cup. 2 cookies for $1.00." Joey had printed a picture of a manatee from the computer, and Katy had pasted it on the sign. At the bottom of the sign in smaller letters, it read "Tips and donations accepted."

"The tips and donations was my idea," Bobby said proudly.

"Looks like you kids have made this a real family project," their mother said.

Grandma brought a tray of cookies out to the table and placed a clear cake cover over them to keep the bugs off. The day before she and Katy had made peanut butter cookies, snickerdoodles, and an old family favorite, corn-flake cookies. Grandpa brought an ice chest and placed it under the table. Cups, napkins, and a large pitcher of lemonade completed the inventory. Katy was in business.

Joey and Bobby gathered up buckets, rags, window cleaner, and hoses. They set up shop on the far side of the driveway, so they wouldn't get anyone wet. Their grandfather had bought them a special nozzle for the hose so it wouldn't waste any water. He also got them some bio-degradable detergent.

"We need to do our part to be as green as we can be," he said.

"What do you mean about being green?" Bobby said.

Grandpa explained that being green means doing things that are friendly to the earth, like recycling, using energy-efficient appliances, not polluting the air or water, and protecting our existing natural resources.

"So instead of Goonies, like in the movie *The Goonies*, we can be The Greenies," Bobby said.

They all laughed.

"Hey, I could write my own movie," he continued. "It would be about a bunch of kids who save the earth from pollution, litter, and bad guys. They'd all wear green capes and carry special zappers which I would invent, and they'd zap people who did things that are bad for the earth, the ocean and rivers, and animals. They could…"

"You could get busy, because our first customer just pulled up," Joey said. "First you have to wash a few cars. Then you can save the world."

"Right," he said.

But Joey knew they hadn't heard the end of The Greenies idea.

Chapter 15
A Surprise Visitor

By mid-afternoon they had earned more than the $25 they needed to adopt a manatee. Bobby had to leave for his baseball game. Joey put all the car wash equipment away, and offered to sit with Katy. She wanted to continue selling lemonade and cookies until they were all finished.

They were busy counting their money when a SUV with an out-of-state license tag pulled into the driveway. Joey started to walk over to the car to tell them that the car wash was over, but then stopped abruptly. The back door of the vehicle opened and a blond girl jumped out.

"Surprise!" she said. And he was surprised. It was Barby.

She ran over to him and then stopped suddenly, not knowing quite how to greet him. "Gotcha," she said.

Joey was speechless. He didn't know what to say. He finally gained his composure and said, "What are you doing here? And how did you find our house?"

"I came to see you, silly. And I had your address, so we put it into our GPS system, and voila. Here we are!"

Joey's mother came out of the house when she saw their car in the driveway. Joey, still in a bit of shock, looked at his mother and then said, "Mom, you remember the Masons. We met them last year in St. Augustine."

"Of course," she said. "Joey told me you might be visiting Florida again. What a nice surprise."

Yeah, thought Joey. *This is a real surprise.*

"Why don't you come in? Have you been traveling long?"

Barby's parents had gotten out of the car and were stretching. They shook hands with Jennifer and followed her into the house. Laurie, Barby's little sister, walked over to Katy and asked what she was doing. Katy explained her business enterprise and why she was doing it.

"That's really cool," Barby said to Joey. "Did she do this all by herself?"

"No, my brother and I did a car wash, too. But he had a baseball game this afternoon, so we shut down about an hour ago. I was sitting with Katy, so my mom could get some housework done. My grandparents took Bobby to his game."

"Are you really raising money to adopt a manatee?" she said.

Joey was a little embarrassed. He nodded his head sheepishly.

"I think that's wonderful,"she said. "What a neat idea. Laurie, go ask dad for some money so we can buy some cookies and lemonade."

Joey finally started to relax. "So how long are you going to be here?"

She explained that her parents had rented a condo in St. Augustine. They were planning to be there for a week. She said she talked her dad into stopping by his house on their way to St. Augustine, so she could surprise Joey.

"Were you surprised?"

"Ah, yeah. I had no idea you were coming."

"Good. A girl's got to keep her boy friends on their

toes," she said, and then added quickly, "I mean friends that are boys, like…you know what I mean, don't you?"

Joey grinned. "Yeah, I know what you mean." And he felt a lot better, knowing that she felt a little awkward too.

He convinced Katy to close up shop, so they could all go inside. Most of the cookies were gone, and there would be just enough lemonade for the four of them to have a cool drink. The adults were in the living room, and Joey's mom was telling Barby's parents about their

favorite things to do in St. Augustine.

"Maybe you and the kids can come down and meet us for dinner one night," Barby's father said.

"That would be nice," Jennifer said.

"How about tomorrow?" Mrs. Mason said.

"Actually, I was planning on taking the kids up to Jekyll Island to the Georgia Sea Turtle Center tomorrow. Maybe your girls would like to go with us? And we could all meet for dinner afterwards," she said.

"Oh, can we?" Laurie whined.

Barby's parents looked at each other, shrugged their shoulders, and agreed. Barby looked at Joey and grinned.

This investigation is going to be the best one yet, Joey thought. *Who'd have thought that sea turtles could be so exciting?*

Chapter 16
Sea Turtles

The next morning was Sunday. The Johnson family went to the first church service, so they could get an early start on their trip to Jekyll Island. The Masons met them at a fast food restaurant for lunch. Barby and Laurie were excited about spending the day with their Florida friends. And their parents were looking forward to having an afternoon alone to explore some of the historic sights of St. Augustine.

Bobby jumped in the front seat of the family minivan, knowing this time he wouldn't have to fight for it. Joey and Barby took the middle seat, and Katy and Laurie crawled into the far back seat. The little girls had become instant friends and found many things to talk about. Giggles were a large part of their conversations.

Joey and Barby were discussing the Mason's last-minute trip. Barby explained that they discovered on very short notice that her dad had been selected to attend this conference, and they had been lucky to get accommodations.

"I would have let you know, but we left very quickly," she said. "We only had two days' warning, and we had to go shopping for some summer clothes. Plus, I thought it would be fun to surprise you. You don't mind, do you?"

Joey gave her a scolding look, but then smiled. "Nah, it's OK. It was a good surprise."

Then they talked about school and sports and their plans for the next year. Both would be entering high school in the fall. Barby admitted that she was a little nervous about it. Joey was glad to know that he wasn't alone.

As they drove north on Interstate 95, Jennifer explained where they were going. She told them the Georgia Sea Turtle Center had been built to provide emergency care to sick and injured sea turtles. Several species of sea turtles build their nests along the southeastern coast of the United States. Sometimes these turtles get struck by boats, or caught in fishing nets, or become victims of pollution in the ocean. Injured turtles can be brought to the Georgia Sea Turtle Center for medical treatment and rehabilitation.

"How do they treat them?" Laurie asked.

"Oh, you'll see. They have veterinarians, a hospital, and special rehabilitation tanks where the turtles can stay until they get better. They also have some educators and volunteers to show you around and some interactive exhibits where visitors can learn all about the turtles – how they live and grow, and what dangers they face."

The kids had lots of questions, but Jennifer told them to save them for the experts. When they turned off the interstate, they could see the marshes and waterways that surround this South Georgia area. Katy and Laurie started counting the birds they saw. Katy counted the birds that were flying, and Laurie counted birds that were in the water or on land.

Joey had brought his camera and asked his mom if they could stop by the *Welcome to Jekyll Island* sign so he could take a picture of everybody. He took several pictures of the group, and then asked his mother to take one of just him and Barby. Bobby made kissing sounds until his mother made him stop.

After the photo session, they turned onto the two-lane causeway that took them out to Jekyll Island. They could see several pleasure boats enjoying a Sunday afternoon on the water as their van crossed the bridge over the Intracoastal Waterway.

Jennifer explained that the island was not very big. They would go to the Georgia Sea Turtle Center first. Later they could walk around the historic district or go hiking on one of the bike trails. She wanted them to see some of the other sights, both historic and natural, before they left the island.

"This island has some beautiful scenery and lots of wildlife. I have some friends who live here and they tell me they often see deer in their neighborhood," she said.

"Maybe we could see an alligator, too," Bobby said. "How cool would that be?"

The girls in the back squealed. Joey rolled his eyes and shook his head. Jennifer gave Bobby a dirty look.

"You don't have to worry about any alligators, girls," she said. "We won't go anywhere where it's dangerous." She pinched Bobby on the leg and whispered to him to "Cool it."

Jennifer pulled into a parking lot surrounded by huge oak trees. As they started down a sidewalk that led to a large brick building, Katy and Laurie wanted a picture in front of the sign that read *The Georgia Sea Turtle Center.*

"I'm going to make a scrapbook of our trip," Katy said. Laurie said she wanted to make one too. Joey took a pic-

ture of the sign and then another one of the girls in front of the sign. Bobby tried to sneak into the background, but his mother caught him and held him in a big bear hug until the picture was taken. He squirmed like a hungry baby, but she wouldn't let go. Before he escaped her clutches, she gave him a peck on the cheek.

Jennifer paid for their admission. Each of the kids was given a *Sea Turtle Journal* with information about sea turtles and asked questions which could be answered by interacting with the exhibits. A giant sea turtle was hanging above the gift shop. Entering the Exhibit Gallery, they saw large murals with beautiful color photographs of sea turtles. Several life-size sea turtle models were suspended from the ceiling. On one wall was a large glass window that looked into a room that resembled a hospital. And in fact, it was a hospital.

Bobby saw two persons from the veterinary staff tending to a small turtle in the treatment room. Jennifer was helping Katy and Laurie read some of the exhibits and the *Danger* signs posted around the room. One told them there is only a one in four thousand chance that a turtle hatchling will survive to become a mature adult. Many of the turtle eggs are eaten by natural predators like raccoons, birds, and foxes, so many hatchlings never make it to the ocean. And of those that make it to the water, many are eaten by creatures in the sea.

"That's so sad," Laurie said.

"We learned all about this last week when we went to a Research Reserve with my grandparents," Katy said. "The lady told us that there are people who go out on patrols on the beach to protect the turtle nests. When I get older, I'm going to do that."

"I'd like to do that, too," Laurie said.

"She also told us that litter, like plastic things, is a big problem too. The turtles eat it by mistake or they get tangled up in it."

"I don't want to hear any more of that. That's sad. I wanna see some real turtles," Laurie said.

"I know just the place," Jennifer said.

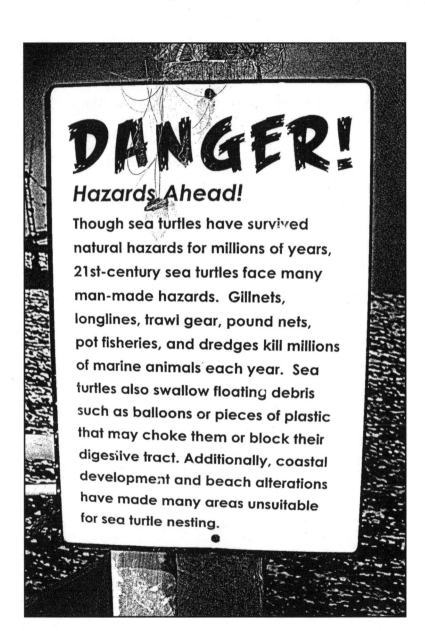

DANGER!

Hazards Ahead!

Though sea turtles have survived natural hazards for millions of years, 21st-century sea turtles face many man-made hazards. Gillnets, longlines, trawl gear, pound nets, pot fisheries, and dredges kill millions of marine animals each year. Sea turtles also swallow floating debris such as balloons or pieces of plastic that may choke them or block their digestive tract. Additionally, coastal development and beach alterations have made many areas unsuitable for sea turtle nesting.

Chapter 17
Saving Sea Turtles

They walked over to the Rehabilitation Pavilion located behind the main building. It was a long wooden structure with screened walls. Inside, were nine round hospital tanks full of water. Some had turtles in them; and some were empty.

One of the Educators was getting ready to give a presentation. Katy and Laurie crowded up near the front so they could see and hear better. Joey, Barby, and Bobby stood behind them.

"Hi, my name is Alicia. Did you guys see that giant sea turtle hanging above the gift shop?" she began. "That was Archelon — a dinosaur sea turtle! That's right. Sea turtles have been around since the time of the dinosaurs. Today all seven species of sea turtles are considered endangered. But with your help, we can

93

ensure that they will be around forever!"

Then she told them about some of their recent patients. She said they usually had two or three turtles there, and sometimes more. Some turtles had to be rehabilitated from injuries after collisions with boat propellers. And others were simply sick, often suffering from dehydration.

Katy raised her hand. "What causes turtles to get sick?"

"There are many things that can make them sick," Alicia said. "The red tide caused by an algae bloom, like they had in Jacksonville recently, can hurt them. And so can marine debris or garbage in the water.

"That's why it's important we all do our part. Even you kids can help. You should pick up garbage, even if it's not yours. And many places now have receptacles for recycling fishing line. So if you see a wad of fishing line somewhere, in or out of the water, you should get rid of it. Otherwise, it could end up hurting one of our friends here."

"What do you do with the turtles when they're all

better?" a boy asked.

"We have to transition them back into the wild, making sure they can feed themselves by finding and capturing live food. We also tag them with a small metal flipper tag, which is kind of like giving the sea turtle an earring. Some turtles get a satellite telemetry transmitter, so we can see where they are going once they leave the Georgia Sea Turtle Center."

She explained that anyone can track these turtles on the Georgia Sea Turtle Center's Web site by clicking on *Patient Updates*.

"Cool," Bobby said to Joey. "Let's do that when we get home."

"Ever since you saw that manatee, you're really getting into this nature stuff, aren't you?" Joey said.

Bobby just shrugged his shoulders, "Yeah, I guess I am. So what? You gonna make fun of me?"

"No, I think it's kinda neat." And he gave his brother a friendly shove.

Alicia told the visitors more stories about injured turtles that had been patients there, and answered a few more questions. She thanked them for visiting and encouraged them to tell their friends about the Georgia Sea Turtle Center.

"We need to educate the public, and especially you kids, about how important it is for all of us to protect these beautiful creatures and the marine ecosystem," she said.

She told them about some of the daily programs they offer, and invited the kids to attend one of their Sea Turtle Camps during the summer. Katy asked her mother if she could attend one of those camps some day. Jennifer said she thought that would be a great idea.

They thanked Alicia, walked back through the Exhibit Gallery, and paused in the gift shop to admire Archelon. Before they left the island, Jennifer drove them around so they could see some of the coastal scenery. They stopped a few times so the kids could do some exploring, and then drove back to Jacksonville.

Chapter 18
Trouble on the River

When they got home that night after dinner in St. Augustine with the Masons, there was a message from their grandfather. He had made a reservation for them on one of the Family River Rides sponsored by the St. Johns Riverkeeper for the following Saturday, but he had gotten a call from their office offering them spaces on a special tour on Tuesday. A summer day camp had scheduled a river tour for its kids and had extra spaces. The Education Coordinator for the Riverkeeper thought they might enjoy taking the tour with other kids.

Joey and Bobby thought that would be fine. Katy wasn't so sure.

"Are they big kids or little kids?" she asked.

"I don't know," her mother said. "I don't think that matters. But I imagine they'll be gearing the activities toward kids, so it will probably be more interesting."

"OK," she said. "I'll go."

Jennifer called her parents to let them know Tuesday would be good. She wouldn't be able to join them, but knew they'd have a good time with another group of kids on board.

They all enjoyed a quiet day on Monday. Jennifer worked on her laptop for most of the morning while the kids were cleaning their rooms. Jennifer bribed them with pizza for dinner if she could see the floor in all of their rooms by the end of the afternoon. That wasn't so difficult for Joey and Katy, but Bobby's room was a disaster. Joey offered to help, and some things actually got put away properly. The rest was shoved under the bed and in the closet. At 4:30, Bobby announced he was hungry and ready to go.

Jennifer did a quick inspection without looking under the bed, and pronounced the rooms reasonably clean. There was a brief discussion about which pizza place to go to, but they all agreed on their favorite Italian restaurant. Bobby asked if they could go over to the County

Dock after dinner, just to see if anyone was catching any fish. When Jennifer agreed, the boys put their fishing poles and tackle box in the back of the van.

After a dinner of salad and pizza, they drove to the riverfront park. Katy took her mother by the hand to give her a tour of the nature walk. She felt very much in-charge, because she had been there before with her grandmother. The boys headed for the dock with all their fishing gear. Jennifer asked Joey to keep an eye on Bobby.

As usual, Bobby stopped to talk to everyone along the

way. No one was catching much, but Bobby was sure he would. He told Joey he wanted to go to the end of the dock, as there was no one there.

"That's my lucky spot," he said. "I saw my first manatee there, so it's special."

When Joey opened the tackle box to get a hook to put on his fishing line, he found a baseball rolling around inside.

"Bobby, you goofball. Why do you have a baseball in your tackle box?"

"I dunno. You never know when you're going to need one."

"That's the stupidest thing I've ever heard you say."

"Nah, you're wrong. I've said a lot dumber things before."

They both laughed. Bobby sat down and dangled his feet over the edge as he worked on his fishing line. Joey had brought his camera and took a picture of Bobby who made a goofy face just as Joey snapped the shot.

Just then a small motor boat with two teenaged boys came buzzing by the dock. The wake of their boat was creating a disturbance and many of the fishermen were yelling at them to go away. The boys in the boat simply laughed at them and made another pass.

As the boat was about to head back out into the river, it circled around, slowed down, and the two boys started pointing into the water. Not far off of the bow of their boat was a large object floating on the surface.

"Oh, my gosh," Bobby cried. "It's a manatee. I hope they're not going to do something stupid."

They watched in horror as the boat circled it several times and then one of the boys started to poke at the slow-moving mammal with a pole. The other one was trying to reach the manatee's flipper.

"Hey, you guys," Bobby yelled. "Stop that! You could hurt it."

The teens in the boat looked at Bobby and just laughed.

"Who's going to stop us, you little twerp?" the bigger boy shouted back.

"Come over here and I will," Bobby answered.

"Bobby, that's not such a good idea. He's probably

twice your size. And I doubt that he plays by any rules," Joey said.

"I don't care. They're going to hurt it."

Some of the people who had been fishing on other parts of the dock joined Joey and Bobby. Joey still had his camera around his neck and so he started taking pictures of the encounter. He had brought his camera hoping to get a picture of a manatee, and this wasn't what he had in mind, but documenting this abuse could prove to be valuable.

"I've seen those hooligans here before," one lady said. "They're always starting some kind of trouble. It's high time we do something about them."

She pulled a cell phone out from her back pocket and dialed a number. She talked to someone, explaining the situation and then hung up. She suggested they try to find a way to keep those boys in the area for awhile. She told them help was on the way.

"But they could hurt that manatee," Bobby said.

"Then we need to distract them, don't we?" she answered.

Several of the others hollered at them too, but they realized it was impossible to make them stop. Joey looked around for his mother, but she was nowhere in sight. *That was probably good*, he thought. *Things could get rough.*

Then Bobby said he had an idea.

"We don't need to just distract them – we need to disable them so they can't get away," he said excitedly. "And I've got a plan."

He explained that they needed to lure them closer to the dock. That would do two things. It would get them away from the manatee, and it would give him a clear shot at them. He reached in the tackle box and pulled out his baseball. He explained that he was pretty good with a baseball and he intended to cause some serious damage to their boat's motor if they came close enough.

"You think you can hit it, Kid?" one of the fishermen said.

"My brother is the best baseball player in his league," Joey said proudly.

Then he asked Bobby if he thought he could really hit it. "If you miss, we better be prepared to run," he said.

"I like it," the lady with the cell phone said. "And you won't have to run because we won't let them do anything to you."

So they plotted quickly and decided the best way to lure them over closer was to insult them. The adults were going to wander back down the dock so it would look like they were no longer interested.

"We won't be far, if you need us," one of the men said. Joey looked at Bobby and asked him again if he was sure he wanted to do it. Bobby nodded his head that he did.

"OK, then I'm with you 100%. Let's do it!"

Bobby took a deep breath. "Hey Fatso, is that your sister swimming in the water next to you?"

"Oh, good grief," Joey said quietly. "You're going to get us killed."

Chapter 19
Bobby and Joey to the Rescue

The two boys in the boat looked at Bobby in astonishment. They weren't used to being challenged or insulted. They talked to each other for a minute and appeared to be arguing. The bigger boy shoved the other kid down in the boat and looked around for the manatee. He started splashing his hands in the water, trying to lure the gentle creature over to the boat.

Manatees sometimes think people will give them food, so they will respond to efforts like this. But this manatee was wary and actually started swimming away from the boat toward the dock.

"C'mon, Big Boy," Joey said quietly. "Come this way."

The watchers on the dock held their breath as the manatee slowly swam away from the boat. Bobby was hoping it would dive deeper and be gone, and it did for a moment. But then it surfaced again, only this time there were two of them.

"Holy cow!" Bobby said. "There's another one."

"Don't you mean Holy Sea Cow?" Joey said. They both laughed, but the humor faded quickly as they heard the boat's engine start up. It was heading in their direction.

"Well, Bobby. Be careful what you wish for, because it looks like you're going to get it."

"Gimme the baseball. I'll hide it behind my back until

they're within range. I'm gonna nail that sucker!"

"I hope so," Joey said, picking up his fishing pole. He felt he needed something in his hands in case Bobby needed defending. A fishing pole was better than nothing. He was not going to let these bullies get to his little brother.

The boat made a circle in the water a short distance from the end of the dock. It was too far away for Bobby to be able to hit the boat's engine.

"Maybe they're just all talk, and they'll go away," Joey said.

"Maybe, but I'm not backing down until they leave," Bobby said. "I couldn't stand it if they did something to those manatees. It's like Grandma said, someone has got to stand up for the animals. And today, I guess it's you and me."

Joey was so proud of his younger brother that he could have hugged him. Of course, that would not be appropriate now, but maybe later. He hoped they'd both still be alive later.

Just then the boat started charging the manatees. Joey

was the first to react.

"Hey, you goons. Why don't you come pick on someone from your own species," he yelled. "Oh, I forgot. We don't have any apes around here." He started sticking his tongue out at them and making punching and kicking gestures.

"You want some of this?" he said, pointing to himself. "Or are you only brave when you have a stick in your hand?"

The boy driving the boat slowed the engine. He looked like he wanted to leave, but the bigger boy urged him to steer toward the dock.

Joey walked to the other side about ten feet away from Bobby. If they came after Joey, it would position the boat broadside so Bobby could get a better shot at the engine. Joey stood there at the end of the dock, signaling the boy to come to him. The closer the boat got, the madder he got.

How dare they, he thought. *Now I know how Bobby feels. We've got to stop them.*

The boat drew closer and closer. By now, Joey was

not even afraid. He just wanted it to happen. *Let's get it over with*, he thought. He didn't dare glance at Bobby as it might give him away. He just kept jeering at the duo.

And then, he heard it. Ka-bam! Bobby had hit the engine dead center. The kid driving the boat almost jumped overboard with surprise. The engine sputtered and stopped. Smoke poured from the back of the boat. Fortunately the current carried the boat away from the dock, so the two trouble-makers were unable to do anything but argue with each other.

"What happened?" the larger boy screamed.

"I dunno. Something happened to the motor. Maybe we hit something."

"Or maybe something hit you," Joey yelled.

The two boys looked around, but still had no idea what had happened. Just then, a marine patrol boat came into view. It was coming straight for them. The lady with the cell phone was waving at the man in the boat. Everyone who had been fishing on the dock joined Bobby and Joey.

"That's the official I called," the lady said. "I've seen

these kids here before and told him about them, but we've never been able to catch them red-handed. If all of you are willing to sign statements, I think we can teach those boys a lesson."

Joey added, "And I have pictures. That should help." Bobby gave him a high-five.

The man on the patrol boat had pulled up alongside the disabled watercraft. He was talking to the lady on her cell phone and shaking his head. After he hung up, he made the two troublemakers get into his boat, tied their boat behind his, waved to the crowd on the dock, and left.

"I need to get all of your names and phone numbers. Someone will be calling you for a statement," she said. They all cheered and patted Bobby and Joey on the back.

Just then Jennifer and Katy joined them.

"What's going on," Jennifer said with concern.

"Oh nothing," Bobby said. "We just took some of Grandpa's advice."

"I don't understand. Are you two OK?" she asked.

"Lady, they're better than OK. They're great!" said

one of the fishermen, and shook Bobby's hand. "You two make a pretty good team."

Bobby grinned. Joey looked embarrassed.

Just then there was a commotion in the water.

"Look, Mom. There's a manatee!" Katy shouted. About twenty feet away from the dock, one of the manatees surfaced. Its head came far enough out of the water for them to see its eyes. It looked at Bobby for a long minute, and then dove back under water.

"I think he was smiling at you, Bobby,"Katy said.

"You think so?"he said.

"Yeah, I know so," Joey said. And the two brothers draped their arms around each other as the crowd was growing around them.

Chapter 20
The River Tour

During their ride home, Bobby told his mother and Katy everything that had happened. Joey sat quietly as Bobby gave colorful details of the encounter. Jennifer kept looking at Joey for reassurance, but all Joey did was nod in agreement and allowed his brother to tell the story.

"Well, that sounds pretty incredible," she said. "I'm very proud of both of you, but I wish you'd find a little safer way to become protectors of the earth."

Joey kept thinking about that throughout the next day when they went for their tour of the St. Johns River. Bobby was disappointed because Neil wasn't there, but a pretty lady welcomed them onto the large pontoon boat.

"Hi, I'm Danielle, the Education Coordinator for the St. Johns Riverkeeper. We're going to go up the St. Johns River and into one of its major tributaries, the Ortega.

And we're going to let you kids help perform some tests on the water quality."

The boat headed upstream and Danielle told them the history of the river, from prehistoric animals to the Timucuan Indians and the Civil War. She talked about the plants and animals that make the St. Johns their home.

The boat stopped at one spot and she took some samples of the river water and let the kids help her measure the levels of nitrates and phosphates. She told them many pollutants come from lawn fertilizers. She explained how

the same nutrients that make your yards turn green, also cause algae to grow. As the algae dies, it uses up the oxygen needed by other plants and animals. It also blocks needed sunlight from penetrating the water.

Bobby looked at Joey, and Joey knew what he was thinking. *Just like our fishing pond.*

After they did some more water tests, including checking the temperature and the levels of dissolved oxygen and turbidity of the water, she pronounced the river as being sick. She added that for as long as people have been using the river, they've also been abusing it. She talked about too much storm water run-off, too much water-use, and what it was all doing to the natural habitat.

As they headed back to the dock, Danielle told them, "We all need to help save the river in any way we can. Even if it's only saving a little water each day. You can turn off the water when you're brushing your teeth. And you can take a shorter shower. Every drop of water we use is one less drop for the St. Johns River."

The kids from the summer camp asked lots of

questions, but Joey, Bobby and Katy just sat there. They kept hearing the same story over and over everywhere they went – people were causing many of the problems for the environment.

It was a beautiful sunny summer day on the river. Joey kept thinking about the manatees, and the fish, and the other animals that lived in or near the water, and the impact that human abuse was having on them.

The van was unusually quiet on the way home. Each of them was thinking about what they had seen that day, and what had happened the day before, and how it was all connected to them. Joey spoke first.

"You know, there's got to be something we can do." His words hung in the air like bubbles waiting to pop.

"I was thinking the same thing," Bobby said.

Then Katy added, "We could adopt another manatee."

"We need to DO something," Joey said. "We need to get more active."

That night after supper, Joey went to the computer. He clicked on many of the Web sites of the places they had visited recently, and some others dedicated to the environment. He remembered what the biologist had said at the Research Reserve about protecting the turtles. He revisited the *Save the Manatee* Web site and read the section on *Take Action*. Then he logged onto the *St. Johns Riverkeeper* Web site and went to the page on *How You Can Help*. He downloaded and printed a *River Friend-ly* brochure that gave tips on how to manage your yard without harming the river.

He also remembered the lady who had been taking water samples at the County Dock the first time they went there, so he checked out the *Watershed Action Vol-unteers* page on the Web site for *St. Johns River Water Management District.*

He was struck by the amount of information he found, and felt that if people only knew about all these things, they'd want to do something about it, too. Just then the phone rang. His mother told him it was Barby. He was glad she was calling, but he really wasn't in the mood for chit-chat right now. He had more important things on his mind.

"Watcha doing?" she said in a cheery voice.

"Oh, just checking out some Web sites."

"About what?"

"About a lot of things. Things related to the environment, like protecting animals and our natural resources." There was a long pause. "I guess I'm not very good company tonight. It's just kind of frustrating, because there's so much that needs to be done, but I'm just a kid. I don't feel like I can do anything to help."

Barby was also quiet for awhile. She sensed how serious his mood was, and didn't want to insult him by telling him about the great day she had had at the beach.

"Well, just because you're a kid doesn't mean you can't do something. They always say even one person can make a difference."

"Yeah, I know. But people just don't know about what's happening, and what they should be doing to help. I didn't know a lot of this stuff until we started visiting these places and learning about what's going on, and what we should and should not be doing."

"Then tell them," she said bluntly.

There was a long silence. "What do you mean? Tell who?"

"Tell anyone you can get to listen. Tell your neighbors. Talk to groups. Write a letter to the editor of the newspaper. Start a blog. Join an ecology club at your high school next year. And if your school doesn't have one, start one."

Joey thought about what she was saying. It made perfect sense. What a bozo he was! Why hadn't he thought of that?

"You're right. I can do that. In fact, Bobby and Katy want to do something, too. I bet we can all do that together." Now he was excited. He couldn't wait to tell the others.

"Hey Barby, thanks. Those are all great ideas," he said. And then he remembered his manners. "What did you do today?"

"Oh, not much. We went to the beach, which was incredible. You're so lucky to live in Florida." And then there was an awkward silence. "I was wondering if we were going to be able to see each other again."

"Yeah, I hope so."

"Well, my mom is driving to Jacksonville tomorrow to meet with a lady at the library. They met at a conference last year, so they're going to get together. Would tomorrow be OK?

"Sure. Let me check with my mom, but I think it's going to be OK."

"Great. Call me back and let me know."

"Barby, remind me to tell you what Bobby did yesterday. Well, we both did it, but Bobby was the real hero."

"A hero? If it was something noble, I have a feeling you were a part of it too."

"Well, maybe just a little. Anyway, it's a great story. I can't wait to tell you."

"And I can't wait to hear it." They hung up and Joey went to find his mother.

Jennifer was reading a story to Katy who was falling asleep in her lap. Bobby was on the couch watching a baseball game with Max curled up next to him. Everyone was tired after such an exciting day.

When Joey asked his mother if Barby could visit the

next day, he also told her about Barby's ideas. Jennifer thought they were wonderful and suggested they spend some time the next day brainstorming ways they could get other people involved.

"The main thing is that you need to educate people on what's happening," she said.

"Yeah, I know. Just like we learned about all these problems by visiting these different places. But we can't get everyone to go to these places like we did."

"No, but you can share what you've learned."

Then Bobby added, "We could print some fliers like we did for the lemonade stand and car wash and pass them out to our neighbors. They probably already think we're kinda weird anyway."

"Caring about animals is not weird," Katy said. "Maybe we should do a lecture like the lady at the Reserve."

They all looked at Katy. It wasn't realistic, but it was a good idea.

"Why don't we sleep on it and tackle this issue tomorrow when we're all fresh. A lot has happened today, and everyone looks pretty tired," Jennifer said.

No one argued with her. But Joey knew he would have trouble getting to sleep. Every time he thought about how he and Bobby had taken on those bullies together to protect those manatees, it made him proud. He liked that feeling. He wanted to do more.

Chapter 21
The Greenies

To Katy's delight, Laurie was with her sister when their mom dropped them off the next morning. Barby's mother gave them money to treat everyone to lunch. She said she'd be back later that afternoon.

Jennifer had to go do an interview, but said she'd be back in time to take them to lunch. Their grandparents had come over to stay with them, and Grandma was already in the kitchen making sugar cookies. She had secretly purchased some animal-shaped cookie cutters and wanted to surprise the kids. Usually her five-year-old assistant would help her bake, but today Katy had a guest. So the surprise would not be spoiled.

The kids sat around the kitchen table discussing their newest challenge. Joey explained to everyone what they were trying to accomplish.

"We've got to figure out a way to let people know about the river and other waterways, and what's happening to the animals and the environment."

"We could do a TV commercial," Bobby said.

"Get real. We can't do that," Joey said. "That costs money. Besides we don't have any TV equipment."

"Yes, but we could write something for the newspaper," Barby offered.

"You big kids can do that, but what about us?" Laurie said. "We want to do something, too."

"I liked the idea of doing a flier," Bobby said. "I can deliver them around the neighborhood on my bike."

Katy raised her hand like she was in school. She wanted to talk.

"Why don't Joey and Barby write the words in the flier, and Laurie and I can draw some pictures to go on it. We can draw some manatees, and sea turtles, and birds."

"That's a great idea," Joey said. "I've printed some things from the Internet that I think will help us. We'll get started on the flier. You girls can start drawing some pictures, and Bobby you make a list of places where we can pass them out. Then we'll know how many we need to print."

The grandparents were trying to stay out of it and let the kids develop their own plans, but Grandpa offered to help Bobby make his list. He also said he and Bobby could call a few printing places to see how much it would cost to print them.

"Before we go any further, I think we need a name," Katy said. "What are we going to call ourselves?"

"That's a no-brainer," Bobby said. "We're The Greenies!"

Everyone laughed.

"If that's OK with everyone, then The Greenies it is!" Joey said.

Chapter 22
Kids at Work

Joey and Barby soon realized they had found much more information than they could possibly put in a single flier. They decided to start off with a paragraph about why this was important.

"Let's tell them that we are the next generation and we're concerned about the condition of the planet, specifically what's happening right here," Barby suggested.

"I like that," Joey responded. "Then we can describe some of the issues that we're concerned about — like the quality of the water in the river, and what's happening to the wetlands and the mammals like the dolphins and manatees.

"We can also include the sea turtles and right whales, and tell them what times of the year they are here and reproducing. You know, many people are new to this area and aren't aware of these critical periods."

Barby sorted through some of the pages Joey had printed. "Maybe we should make a list of Dos and Don'ts. That makes it very simple."

"Yeah, and we can give them a list of Web sites to go to or phone numbers of places they can call if they have questions," he added scratching his head. "We definitely have our work cut out for us."

Katy and Laurie came into the office with some drawings of manatees and sea turtles. Barby made a fuss over both of them. Katy reminded them not to forget about adding information about a backyard habitat. Laurie suggested they draw some flowers and butterflies to make that point. The girls left in a rush, anxious to complete their next artistic contribution.

Joey looked at Barby and groaned. "We're going to need more space. How can we tell people everything we want them to know in one-page? Printing can be expensive."

Just then Bobby burst into the room. "Here I am to save the day," he sang.

"Bobby, can't you just enter a room like a normal person?" Joey said.

"But I'm not normal. I'm way above normal. I'm exceptional," he bragged. "Of course, in this case I had some help from Grandpa."

"So tell us, Oh Exceptional One, how are you going to save the day?" Joey asked.

"Grandpa and I made a list of places where we could pass out our fliers. We have over a hundred homes in our subdivision. There are many other neighborhoods around us, and we could even pass them out at the grocery store on a Saturday morning.

"Then we called several printers, and found out that it won't be cheap to print them, especially if we want color copies which we thought we should have with Katy and Laurie's drawings. But Grandpa got talking to one of the printers and told him what we were doing and the man actually offered to print them for free. Can you believe that? We still have to pay for the paper, but that just saved us a ton of money."

Joey grinned at Barby, and then slapped his brother

on the back. "You're not all bad, you know. Tell Grandpa thanks."

"Ah, I did something else too," he said sheepishly. "Now our neighbors are going to think we're really weird, but who cares. It's worth it."

"What did you do now?" Joey asked sarcastically.

Bobby signaled them to follow him outside. In their front lawn was a sign in dark bold letters that said *Do Not Feed the Algae*.

"I saw it on that *River Friendly* brochure you printed. I thought it might get some attention. Then when people ask us about it, we can tell them what it means." He added, "Grandpa said it was OK, but I still need to check with Mom when she gets home."

Joey and Barby both laughed.

"We'll be weird together," Joey said.

"We better get busy. My mom will be here before you know it and I'll have to go back to St. Augustine," Barby said.

They worked on the contents of the flier for the rest of the morning. Jennifer came home and offered to take them to a fast food restaurant for lunch, but they were anxious to keep working on their project, so they settled for peanut butter and jelly sandwiches at home. Barby said they'd contribute the money their mother had given them for lunch to the printing costs.

After lunch, Jennifer reviewed what they had written and made a few suggestions. She also offered to help them do the layout of the flier using some special software on her laptop.

They had it just about finished when Barby's mother returned. Jennifer invited her in for coffee and fresh-baked cookies. Katy and Laurie were excited about the animal shapes. Bobby was more interested in the cookies.

"These are Super-Duper, Grandma!" Bobby said. "I think I'll have some more."

Joey and Barby took their cookies back to the office to begin proofreading the flier. It had the animal pictures on the front side and described the need for preservation efforts to protect these creatures. They directed the readers to Web sites about how to adopt a manatee or sea turtle, and how they could join organizations that are working to protect and preserve the environment. They also listed phone numbers for those organizations, and encouraged them to buy license tags for their cars that would support these efforts.

The back page was sprinkled with flowers, birds, and butterflies and had a list of Dos and Don'ts for homeowners. These included information about using safe fertilizers and pesticides, not over-watering their lawns, and creating low-maintenance landscapes in the yards. They also suggested Web sites about establishing a Wildlife Habitat, being more energy efficient, and recycling.

"I think it looks good," Barby said.

"Yeah, me too," Joey said. "I wish we could do more, but this is a start."

"It's a good start. I think when adults see this coming from kids, they'll pay more attention to it. I just wish I was going to be here when you pass them out. Will you let me know how it goes?"

"Of course," and then he added. "I wish you didn't have to leave so soon."

"Me, too."

Her mother called that it was time to go. She said they would stop by on Saturday on their way home and say goodbye. The conference would be over at noon, so they would be heading north right after lunch.

Joey didn't want to think about them leaving, but he knew they had to go back sometime.

"Thanks for letting us spend the day here," Laurie said to Jennifer, as they were walking out to the car. "It was so much fun."

"You're very welcome. I hope you'll come back again."

Barby thanked her too, and then asked Joey to call her later. He promised he would. Before he knew it, she was gone.

Jennifer put her arm around her eldest son. "She's a nice girl, isn't she?"

"Yeah. Too bad she lives in Boston," he said, and walked dejectedly into the house.

Chapter 23
Making News

The fliers came back from the printer much faster than they expected. In fact, they were able to pick them up on Friday afternoon.

"Let's start passing them out tomorrow," Bobby said. "I don't have a game until 3:00."

"Works for me," Joey said. "I think we need to do this door-to-door so they can see who we are. Besides, it's illegal to put things in the mailbox."

"I wanna go," Katy said.

"Sure," Joey said.

Jennifer added that an adult would need to be with them. She said she'd join them, and it would be good exercise to walk with them.

"Hey, it will be just like Halloween," Bobby said. "Only we won't get any candy."

"This will be better," Katy said. "We'll be doing it for a good cause."

So at 9:00 a.m. sharp, they left the house with a satchel full of fliers. Jennifer thought some people might still be sleeping, so they knocked gently on each door. If no one was home, they left a flier on the front porch. They had signed their first names and their phone number and called themselves "The Greenies."

Some people were working in their yards, so it was easy to talk to them. One man remembered them as the kids who did the car wash so they could adopt a manatee. He wanted to know if they had raised enough money. Joey told him they had and there was information on the flier about how he could adopt one too. He said he'd think about it and thanked them for being concerned about what was happening to the river.

Katy said she wanted to do some talking too, so when an older lady answered at one house, Joey let Katy take charge. The woman was not very friendly at first until Katy complimented her on her flowers. Katy told her that the red ones were especially good for butterflies.

"Yes, dear, I know. But how did you know that?" the older woman said.

"My grandma told me. We're making a backyard habitat so it will be good for the birds and butterflies."

"How nice."

The woman said she'd read the flier and would share it with her garden club. She thought they would be interested in it.

Bobby was going down the other side of the street. Jennifer stayed in the middle, keeping an eye on all of them. Bobby approached a man getting into his car. He gave him a flier and asked him to read it later. The man asked Bobby several questions, and then drove off.

After two hours of walking and talking, they were hot, thirsty, and hungry.

"Let's go home and get something to eat," Jennifer said.

They had just sat down to eat tuna fish sandwiches when the phone rang. Joey answered and grew very quiet. He said "yes sir" several times and then said "just a minute."

"Mom, there's a guy from the TV station who heard about what we're doing. They want to send a TV crew out to interview us. Will that be OK?"

Jennifer looked dumbfounded. "You're kidding?" she said. She got up and took the phone from Joey.

"I'm Mrs. Johnson. May I help you?" She listened mostly and finally said "yes".

She hung up the phone and said, "Better get cleaned up. You're going to be interviewed in about an hour."

"Whoppee," Bobby shouted. "I'm going to be famous."

Katy was clapping her hands. "We have to call Grandma and Grandpa."

"I have to call Barby," Joey said and ran to call her from the phone in the office.

About an hour later, a TV truck pulled up in front of their house. A reporter knocked on the door and introduced himself. Jennifer invited him in and introduced him to the kids. He asked them many questions about how they came up with this idea and why they were doing it.

Bobby told him about seeing a manatee, and raising money so they could adopt one. Katy told about the sea turtles and showed him the backyard habitat. He asked Joey about their campaign, as he called it. Joey said they just wanted to do something. They had visited many places over the past few weeks – the Guana Tolomato Matanzas National Estuarine Research Reserve, the Georgia Sea Turtle Center, the Museum of Science and History, and even went on a Family River Ride on the St. Johns River. They had learned how fragile the river is and they wanted to do something to protect it.

"Adopting a manatee and a sea turtle didn't seem like enough," he said. "So we created theses fliers to try to get other people involved." He showed the reporter one of the fliers.

The reporter kept smiling. He asked Jennifer to sign some release forms so he could interview the kids for the news. She did, and they went outside where he said it would make a better background for their story. He talked to all three of the kids and then to Jennifer. When he had finished interviewing them, he walked through the neighborhood and talked to some of the neighbors. As the cameraman was packing up his gear and loading the car, Bobby asked the reporter when the story would be on TV.

"It should be on the 6:00 o'clock news tonight," he said. "And maybe again at 11:00."

"Oh, good. I have a baseball game at 3:00, but we should be home by 6:00. Maybe you'd like to come do a story on my team?" Bobby said.

"Maybe some other time," the reporter said. "I need to get back and edit this piece so it will be ready in time.

Thanks again for the interview. This is a great story."

As the van started to drive away, the reporter rolled down his window and said, "Keep up the good work. It's nice to be able to tell a good story every now and then."

"Thanks, Mister," Bobby said, and they all waved.

Chapter 24
Making a Difference

A few minutes later Barby's family arrived to say good-bye. Jennifer invited them in, but Mr. Mason said they needed to get on the road. They were going to spend the night in Savannah and he wanted to get there in time to walk around and see some of the historic buildings before it got dark.

Katy wanted to show Laurie the flowers she and her grandmother had planted in the backyard and the birdhouse her grandfather had made for her. Joey and Barby stood by their car, both feeling awkward about saying goodbye.

"I had a really good time this week, especially when we went to Jekyll Island," she said.

"Me too," he mumbled.

"That's so cool about the TV station interviewing you.

You'll have to get a copy and send it to me."

"Sure. Maybe it will get featured on their Web site, too. That would be cool."

"Don't forget my suggestion about writing a letter to the editor of the newspaper, or writing a story yourself. I bet they'd print it," she said.

"I never thought anyone would pay any attention to a bunch of kids, but I was surprised when we passed out the fliers. Many of our neighbors asked good questions. It was kinda cool because I was able to answer most of them," he said. "I just hope they'll read what we put on the fliers." Then he remembered the role she had played in it.

"You know you're the one who had the idea to tell other people. Without you, we wouldn't be on TV to-night. Thanks."

"I'm just glad I could help. I might try to do something like that in my neighborhood. We have many of the same issues in Boston that you have here. I'm going to take one of your fliers home with me."

"You mean YOUR flier," he said.

"No, they're OUR fliers," she replied.

Her father said it was time to go. Laurie had returned from the backyard, gave Katy a hug, and crawled into the car. Barby walked slowly over to the car.

"You folks are going to have to come to Boston to visit us one of these days," Mrs. Mason said. "We'd love to show you the sights. We can even take in a baseball game. I understand you have a Red Sox fan in the family."

Joey grinned. Jennifer said she'd think about that, as she had cousins living outside of Boston.

"And could we go see some whales too?" Katy asked. "My grandma says that's where you can see them."

"Sure," Mr. Mason said. "And we've got a great Aquarium too."

Joey and Barby were both smiling. They liked what they were hearing.

"I gotta go now," she said. She flashed that smile that he had seen the first time he saw her in St. Augustine almost a year ago, and got into the car. "I'll e-mail you."

"That would be great," he said. He didn't know what

else to say. He just stood there, feeling kind of stupid. "Thanks for coming."

She rolled down the window and thanked Jennifer for inviting them to go to Jekyll Island with them. "That was my favorite day of the whole week," she said.

Mine too, thought Joey. And they all waved as they drove off.

Bobby reminded them he had a game to go to. Jennifer knew Joey was a little sad because Barby had left, so she asked him if he'd mind sitting with her at Bobby's game. He didn't want to stay home alone, so he agreed.

Bobby's team won 5-4, and as usual he scored one of their runs. He was hot and sweaty and dirty afterwards. He usually had more dirt on his uniform than any of the other players. Jennifer bought hot dogs for everyone from the concession stand, so they could get home quickly to see the 6:00 news. She also called her parents on her cell phone and invited them to come over to watch the news with them.

The evening news had several stories at the beginning about a house fire, a bad car accident, and an oil spill just north of the city. The newscaster used that as a lead-in to their story.

"And when we come back, we're going to tell you about some youngsters who are trying to protect our waterways," the newscaster said, and everyone cheered.

They waited nervously as the commercials rolled across the television screen.

When the news returned, the newscaster introduced the reporter who had interviewed them earlier. The reporter said this was a story that made him feel good all over. He described a local family who was trying to make a difference.

First he showed the comments from three of their neighbors. One lady said how impressed she was that these young people were getting involved. Another lady said she learned some new things from their fliers and she intended to make some changes at her house. And an older man said he wished more young people were involved in things like this instead of playing video games all day. They all laughed.

Then Bobby's face was on the screen. "I got mad when

I saw all the dead fish in our fishing pond. And then I saw a manatee down at County Dock, and wanted to do something to help protect them."

Katy's interview was next. "It was my idea to do a lemonade stand to earn some money so we could adopt a manatee. My brothers washed some cars, and we earned enough to adopt a sea turtle too. And my Grandma and me made a backyard habitat for birds and butterflies. Wanna see it?"

The cameraman had taken some video of the backyard. During the video of their backyard, the reporter talked about composting and watering lawns only twice a week.

Then Joey was asked how this all got started. "My grandparents are to blame," he said with a grin. "When we were upset about the fish kill, they suggested we visit some places that would help us understand more about the local ecosystem."

The reporter asked them where they went. "We went to the Guana Tolomato Matanzas National Estuarine Research Reserve, the Museum of Science and History downtown, the Georgia Sea Turtle Center on Jekyll Island, and even took a river tour on the St. Johns with the Riverkeeper."

"And what did you learn?" the reporter asked.

"We learned about the quality of water, how it affects the animals, birds, and fish that depend on it, and what people are doing to it. That's when we decided to do the fliers. My friend Barby helped us design them. My little sister and her friend did the art work for it, and my brother Bobby helped us pass them out to our neighbors. Oh yeah, my mother went with us too."

"Do you have any plans to expand your campaign?" the reporter said.

"We'd like to, because we want to reach as many people as we can."

In her interview Jennifer told him how proud she was of her kids. The reporter closed his segment by saying he, too, was proud of these kids. He held up one of the fliers and said, "If you would like to get a copy of one of these fliers, you can go to our station's Web site and obtain a copy to help The Greenies reach more people than they ever thought possible."

When the segment was over, the family applauded and cheered. Bobby gave high-fives all around the room. Their grandparents were smiling and hugging each kid. Jennifer jumped up to answer the phone which had started to ring. It rang throughout the rest of the evening. Many friends called to say they had seen the story on the news. The editor from the newspaper called and said he was interested in a doing a story. Joey asked if he would like him to write something. The editor liked that idea and asked him to e-mail him something on Monday.

Then the Riverkeeper called and asked to speak to Bobby. He congratulated them on helping to get the word out. "You kids have a very special message, and it appears people are listening to you. Keep up the good work."

After Bobby hung up, he announced he was thinking about writing his life's story. "I could sell it to a book company and make millions of dollars. Then I could adopt all kinds of animals."

His grandfather said, "Aren't you the same kid who said he wasn't interested in books just a few days ago?"

Bobby thought about that for a minute. "Yeah, but that was before. Things are different now. Now I have something I care about. That makes a big difference."

"Learning about all these things is what made a difference," his grandfather said.

"Yeah, I know. Thanks for taking us to all those places," he said. And then he added, "Just think. This all started with a bunch of dead fish."

Grandma spoke up. "We've still got the whole summer ahead of us. There's a lot more to see and do. But for now, it's time for us to go home." They gave hugs and kisses all around, told the kids again how proud they were of them, and left.

The house finally became quiet. Katy was almost asleep on the couch, and even Bobby had slowed down. Jennifer shooed them off to bed.

"You've had a very big day today. It's time to re-charge your batteries, too."

"Mom, do you mind if I work on the computer for a little while? I want to get started on this story while it's fresh in my mind."

"Sure, just don't stay up too late. We have church in the morning."

He logged onto the computer, and to his surprise there were dozens of e-mails. The TV station had forwarded them to him. As he read through many of the e-mails, he saw some from interested viewers, a few from some teachers, and one from an environmental group. Some were from kids who wanted to form a Greenies group in their neighborhood.

Reading the e-mails made him feel good. But despite the excitement and sense of accomplishment he felt, he had a nagging feeling that it wasn't enough. The more he learned about the protection of these animals and the preservation of the environment, the more he realized there was so much more to do.

Instead of working on his story, he decided to make a list of some more things he could do. He thought about volunteering with some environmental groups. He could work on some of the clean-up days for the river and the beaches. He liked the idea of starting a blog. He'd call the high school on Monday to see if they have an ecology club. If not, he'd spend some time this summer getting information on how to start one. And he could help start some Greenie groups for other kids.

He decided he'd ask Bobby and Katy to help him develop a list of ways that kids could get involved, and that made him excited just thinking about it.

Maybe he was wrong about kids being able to make a difference. Maybe it was the one group that really could.

THE END

Resources

Georgia Sea Turtle Center
214 Stable Road
Jekyll Island, Georgia 31527
(912) 635-4444
www.georgiaseaturtlecenter.org

Guana Tolomato Matanzas National Estuarine Research Reserve
505 Guana River Road
Ponte Vedra Beach, Florida 32082
(904) 823-4500
www.gtmnerr.org

Museum of Science and History
1025 Museum Circle
Jacksonville, Florida 32207
(904) 396-6674
www.themosh.org

National Wildlife Federation
11100 Wildlife Center Drive
Reston, Virginia 20190
1-800-822-9919
www.nwf.org
www.nwf.org/gardenforwildlife

Save the Manatee Club
500 N. Maitland Avenue
Maitland, Florida 32751
(407) 539-0990
www.savethemanatee.org

St. Johns Riverkeeper, Inc.
2800 University Blvd. North
Jacksonville, Florida 32211
(904) 256-7591
www.stjohnsriverkeeper.org

About the Author

Jane R. Wood was born in Astoria, Oregon, but moved to Florida when she was ten. She grew up near the Kennedy Space Center, witnessing America's early journeys into space. She graduated from the University of Florida, and taught middle school and high school English for six years. She also wrote for a local newspaper.

In 1988, she earned a Masters degree from the University of North Florida, and spent the next twelve years producing educational television programs for the cable television company in Jacksonville, Florida.

In 2004, her first juvenile fiction book, *Voices in St. Augustine*, was released. *Adventures on Amelia Island: A Pirate, a Princess, and Buried Treasure* was published in 2007. *Trouble on the St. Johns River* continues the escapades of the Johnson family.

Mrs. Wood and her husband, Terry, live in Jacksonville, Florida, near the St. Johns River. She has two grown sons who also live in Jacksonville.

You can visit her Web site at www.janewoodbooks.com.